DEFENSE WINS!!

A NEW, WINNING APPROACH TO TEAM MAN-TO-MAN BASKETBALL

BILL HAUBRICH

PARKER PUBLISHING COMPANY
West Nyack, New York 10995

Library of Congress Cataloging-in-Publication Data

Haubrich, Bill.
  Defense wins! : a new, winning approach to team man-to-man
   basketball / Bill Haubrich.
    p. cm.
   Includes index.
   ISBN 0-13-203720-3
  1. Basketball—Defense. 2. Basketball—Coaching. I. Title.
GV888.H38 1992
796.323'2—dc20   92-13315
                                                              CIP

ISBN 0-13-203720-3

Parker Publishing Company
Business Information Publishing Division
West Nyack, NY 10995

Simon & Schuster. A Paramount Communications Company

Printed in the United States of America

About the Author

BILL HAUBRICH received his B.A. from Plymouth State College and his M.A. in education from Antioch Graduate School, both in New Hampshire. He has been the boys' basketball coach at Concord (New Hampshire) High School since 1980. During that time, Coach Haubrich has turned a struggling program into a consistent winner, with his teams reaching the state's Final Four three of his last five seasons. In 1987, he guided Concord High School to its first championship in twenty-five years with a 19-4 overall record. (Concord's last championship had been in 1962 when the team was coached by his father, Bill Haubrich, Sr.)

Prior to rebuilding the program at Concord, Coach Haubrich served as head coach at Kingswood (New Hampshire) Regional High School where he led that program to its first tournament appearance in thirteen years.

Coach Haubrich is a former president of the New Hampshire Basketball Coaches Association and a current member of the New Hampshire State Basketball Committee. In 1986, he was named Coach of the Year by his peers and was inducted into the Plymouth State Athletic Hall of Fame.

Dedication

To my two coaches: my mother and father
To my supportive teammates: my wife Sherry
and my children Katie, Kris, and Billy

About This Book

Growing as a basketball coach is a neverending process. There is an ongoing quest for the unstoppable offense and the impenetrable defense, but to my knowledge, neither has been devised yet. The search goes on. I have experimented with many offenses and defenses in my thirteen years of coaching at the high school level and still look to other coaches for tips, ideas, or drills that might fit into our scheme of things and help to improve us in some way.

After many years of trial and error, we have established a defensive system that works—a system that I would like to share with coaches who are looking for ways to improve themselves. This system, based on combining the strengths of man-to-man and zone defense into a team man-to-man concept, is now the fundamental structure of our successful program.

Bringing man-to-man concepts together with zone concepts to formulate a combination man-zone defense is certainly not a new idea. Many coaches have used this philosophy to promote an aggressive style of defensive play. The one common complaint, however, has been that its success requires five very quick players—not a luxury that most teams have year in and year out. With this in mind, I have modified this defensive system to the point where position, and not quickness, is the determining factor in its success.

This book presents the philosophy and principles upon which our "team man-to-man" system is built. You will find that it is conventional in some aspects, unique in others, but consistent in its expectations to make it logical, and thus attainable, for the players. We have used this defense with small, quick teams as well as with tall, slow ones. As hoped, the "team man-to-man" defense worked equally well with both. As long as I coach high school basketball and continue to have little control over the size and athletic ability of the players in the program, this defensive system will remain the cornerstone of my program.

In this era of basketball where the three-point shot is developing into a potent, destructive offensive weapon, man-to-man is the logical defense to play. Pressure on the ball is much more intense in the man-to-man situation than in the zone, and outside shooting percentages noticeably decline when shooters are consistently challenged. However, straight man-to-man defense does present liabilities that can be exploited by the offense. With this in mind, we have combined the elements of man-to-man defense with zone concepts into a defense that pressures the ball in the man-to-man format and supports off the ball like a zone.

To help our players master the "team man-to-man" system, we teach it to them in a series of fundamentals and rules. All fundamentals that we use have been broken down and explained to the slightest detail, with diagrams and drills included to help show how we present each of them to our players. Although our rules are few in number, we consider them the backbone of our defense and demand that our players execute each and every one. These rules are discussed thoroughly: for every rule there is an explanation of why it has been instituted and how it is best taught, together with diagrams for the coach and drills for the players.

Using the "team man-to-man" philosophy we have extended our defense full court and added trapping and rotation to put unyielding pressure on our opponents. Although this provides a different look to our defense—one that has provided us with much success since its origination—the fundamentals and rules are surprisingly consistent to our halfcourt system, and we have found that the few added responsibilities are easily processed and carried out by our players. These added fundamentals and rules have been included along with the drills that we use to help teach this facet of our defense.

Defense Wins!!! provides the basketball coach with the ultimate weapon—a practical and proven defensive approach that really works. The defensive system that is explained in this book has turned our once struggling program into a consistent winner. Since its inception seven years ago, seven straight winning seasons have ensued with three of our last five teams reaching the state semi-finals, highlighted by a state championship in 1987. Before the "team man-to-man," this program had suffered through five straight losing seasons and only one semi-final appearance in twenty-three years. I am confident that this defensive system can turn any program into a winner as well as enhance an already successful one.

If there is one observation that I can make with thirteen years of coaching under my belt it is this: It's no coincidence that teams that win championships play good defense. On the following pages are ideas that not only have helped us, but may help you to lead your team to greater success.

Bill Haubrich

Contents

Chapter Three
TEACHING THE FUNDAMENTALS OF THE TEAM MAN-TO-MAN DEFENSE 41

Chapter Five
TEACHING THE FULL-COURT PRESS 121

Chapter Six
PRESENTING THE FULL-COURT PRESS TO THE PLAYERS 147

AFTERWORD 181

ONE

DEVELOPING A COACHING PHILOSOPHY

Coaching basketball poses quite a challenge when you consider all the facets of the game that must be covered. Individual players must be schooled in the finer points of the game, while at the same time teams must be prepared to work together within the coach's system. This system is based on an offensive and defensive philosophy that is structured around the talent of the athletes in the program. With each graduating class comes a change in talent that forces the coach to reevaluate his coaching system on a yearly basis.

In the thirteen years I have spent as a varsity coach at the high school level, I have seen a lot of talent come and go. During my younger, learning years as a coach, I felt compelled to revamp the program each year in an attempt to take advantage of returning strengths and cover up probable weaknesses. In the process I experimented with many offenses and defenses, and our style ranged from an uptempo, "run and gun" team that averaged 75 points a game to a deliberate, hold-the-ball-for-a-good-shot team that averaged only 46 points per game. Those styles, I felt, fit in best with the talent on hand.

1

After five years of reshaping the program I came to the realization that the only consistency in our program was inconsistency. Returning players weren't necessarily experienced players since they had to fit into a different system the next year. The coaches of our "feeder" teams were unsure as to how to prepare their players for the varsity team. Our players, veterans of different styles of play, were comparing the different systems and questioning why some moves were made. The success of our program took a decided turn for the better when, after six years, I felt secure enough to determine a style of play that was best for the players in our system, that was best for me as a coach, and that was one that the players could adjust to instead of vice-versa. In the seven years that have followed, the success of our program has soared.

DEFENSIVE EFFICIENCY

There are two basic ways for a coach to approach this game. One is to prepare the team to outscore the opposition by concentrating on the offensive skills of his players. The other is to try to hold opponents to less points by emphasizing the importance of defense. Realistically, a coach's philosophy will end up somewhere between these two approaches, but it rarely lands right in the middle—coaches view the importance of offense and defense in varying degrees.

After experimenting with both, I see the approach that emphasizes defense as the one with more potential for success. Its implementation alone calls for a team effort to produce positive results. Offensive-minded teams often rely on one or two players to carry the load, while defensive-structured teams depend upon team efforts. In our program I have witnessed that although close games are decided by big baskets, the opportunity for those shots goes, more often than not, to the team playing the better defense. I have also noticed that the bigger the game, the lower the scores, indicating that pressure seems to enhance the defensive effort and negatively affect offensive performance. To me the choice is clear. Develop a team that is fundamentally sound on defense, one that takes pride in stopping the opponent, and you will have a team that will shine in "crunch time" and have a chance to win every time they take the floor.

I can say these words with confidence because our program became competitive throughout the state when the commitment was made to defense as the number one priority. At one time I thought that good defense meant holding the ball and keeping the score low. Now I realize that defense is more than a statistic, it is the foundation of a winning program. In our locker room we have only one sign, and it reads, "DEFENSE WINS!!!" Our kids have bought into this philosophy, and they bond together to do the job at the defensive end of the court. The mental and physical effort, sense of cooperation, and team pride that develops in this joint effort have created an atmosphere where our players have confidence in one another—and this helps us with all facets of the game.

OBJECTIVES OF EFFECTIVE DEFENSE

My early experiments taught me that in order for my team to be effective on defense, the following objectives must be met:

1. There must be constant pressure on the ball.
2. Dribble and pass penetration to the basket must be prevented.
3. Passing the ball must be made difficult.
4. Rebounding position must be obtained on every shot.

A breakdown in any one of these areas marked a weakness in our defense and provided the offense with advantageous scoring opportunities. I found that a traditional man-to-man ("always stay between your man and the basket") was efficient at putting pressure on the ball, but fell short in preventing quicker opponents from penetrating to the hoop. Passing was made difficult when we added the "ball-you-man" philosophy, but players were often caught out of position when it came to rebounding. Zones, on the other hand, did a nice job of preventing the ball from penetrating to the basket, but gave up uncontested outside shots due to lack of pressure on the ball. We rebounded better because our players were closer to the basket, but passing for our opponents was no trouble and they easily attacked at their own pace. The obvious answer was to combine the strengths of both defenses into one defensive system. We have done that with the team man-to-man defense. We now challenge our players to play aggressive man-to-man while at the same time providing zone backup with weak-side players sagging to the middle. Not only do we meet the four objectives already listed, but we've come across several other advantages as well.

1. The whole team is involved.   The player's responsibility in the team man-to-man system is not to keep his man from scoring, but to keep the other team from scoring. In order to put pressure on the ball, prevent penetration to the basket, make passing difficult, and secure rebounding positions, all five players on the court must contribute. If one player fails, the system fails.

2. Pressure wears down opponents.   Teams are often used to having their own way bringing the ball downcourt and setting up their offense away from the basket. They are met by defensive pressure when they approach the scoring area and there the concentration begins. A team man-to-man defense forces extra concentration as there is always pressure on the ball. This often causes the offensive effort to deteriorate as the game wears on. We have found that the further we extend our defense away from the basket, the more wear and tear we create on the opposition both mentally and physically, and the more effective our defense becomes with each successive possession.

3. Takes away the three-point shooter.   The three-point shot has become an effective weapon for many high school teams. Zones are often victimized by skip passes that set up wide open attempts from three-point range. The pressure on the ball that comes about through man-to-man makes it difficult for the good shooter to open up for an uncontested shot from the outside. Our team uses the three-point shot as much as any team in our division and we have found that its success is dramatically limited by man-to-man defense. Zones allow our players to shoot off the pass and follow through to the basket—ideal conditions for the long range shot. Man-to-man defense causes our players to create an opportunity from three-point range, and often this results in a shot off the dribble or one falling away from the basket making the shot a low percentage one. Our players know that we can limit our opponents' three-point effectiveness with good, on-the-ball defense.

4. The defense is active, not passive. Most zones are passive defenses. They call for players to stand around with their hands up in a design to keep the ball out of the middle. This defensive style is often vulnerable because it allows the offense to make calculated decisions and to set the tempo of their choice. Our man-to-man approach challenges the offense to make quick decisions and the tempo of play is greatly affected by the defensive intensity. This active approach is often mirrored at the offensive end with all five players making spirited contributions to the offensive effort. Many times a team's offensive woes can be related to a lack of intensity at the defensive end.

5. Allows us the opportunity to win every game we play. Solid defense is often the key to victory. Relying on offensive output to defeat opponents is dangerous because cold shooting, foul trouble to key personnel, and other hard-to-control factors can have an effect on offensive performance. The defensive effort is a more consistent weapon. Man-to-man is the late-game defense forced on teams that have fallen behind. We have confidence in our comeback ability because we are playing the defense we work on every day in practice. Fourth-quarter deficits are lethal to zone-oriented teams: they have little choice but to use their secondary defense in an attempt to catch up.

6. Man-to-man defense is the foundation of all defenses. All defensive schemes have their roots in man-to-man skills. Good man-to-man players fit into any defensive system. Zones and match-ups specify areas in which players must play man-to-man. By developing these individual skills on a daily basis in our program, we can implement an effective zone with little trouble. Zone-based teams generally do not play good man-to-man.

EMPHASIZING DEFENSE

I have tried to develop a team concept into my program. One early lesson that I learned was the vulnerability of building a team around one or two players. Cold shooting nights, foul trouble, or injuries spelled doom to such teams, and petty jealousies often sprung up from those doing the "dirty work" without getting any of the headlines. Individuals seem to create adversity; teams overcome it. In order to develop the team concept in each of my players, I found that this was best done by emphasizing defense. Our players know that they are going to work on defense every day in practice, and they are expected to contribute to the effort. There are no stars on defense, only five hardworking parts, so players must sacrifice their identity to be part of the system. With all five players actively contributing to a common objective, confidence and compatibility are built into the system. The end result is a team effort which is much more productive than individual efforts.

IMPLEMENTING THE DEFENSE

Making the choice to emphasize the team man-to-man defense is just the beginning of commitment. The coaches and players in the system must not merely understand this decision—they must be willing to work hard to make the system work. This is easier said than done. Coaches have long been conditioned to view offensive skills as basketball ability. Players chosen for teams are often the twelve best offensive players, with defensive ability only an afterthought. It may take an adjustment for some coaches in the program to realize that inconsistent shooters or mediocre ball-handlers can contribute positive qualities to a winning program. Even the players themselves have been psychologically affected by the perception that offense is everything. They see the public and media dwell on offensive performance and label those with scoring touches as the game's "best." Michael Jordon is a good example. He excels at both ends of the court, yet it is his offensive skill that is highlighted and written about. Players have to see below the surface of this game and realize the importance of defense. They must understand that in order for the team to succeed, defensive skills must be nurtured and mastered. Offense gets the publicity; defense wins championships.

THE COACH'S ROLE

No doubt the head coach is the catalyst who will make this system work. He not only has to design a plan to teach his team how to play with defensive skill, but he must also convince his players to want to play defense. This becomes more of a process than a plan, and to the coach aspiring to institute an effective team man-to-man defense into his program I offer the following six pieces of advice:

1. Be knowledgeable.   Study the fundamentals of man-to-man defense and then learn how to best coordinate these fundamentals into this defensive system. A knowledgeable coach is a confident one, and this confidence will carry over to the players in your program. Don't be afraid to expand your horizons beyond personal playing experiences. Watch good defensive teams play, observe other coaches teaching defense at practice or at camps, converse with other coaches and listen to their ideas, keep an open mind at clinics, and read books that address the subject. Gather all the information you can on defense and then use what you feel is best for you and best for your team.

2. Be a teacher.   Successful coaches not only know the game, but they are able to communicate that knowledge to their players. In developing a team that plays team man-to-man, all players must be taught individual defensive techniques. These fundamentals must be separately explained and demonstrated, then drilled until they are thoroughly understood and properly executed. This will allow each player to react instinctively to every situation, building the necessary foundation for this defensive system.

3. Be organized.   Teaching all aspects of individual and team man-to-man defense is a monumental task. It is a journey that will reach its destination only through a well-thought-out plan.

Defensive instruction must be a daily occurrence at practice. We have found that scheduling defense early in our practice period is most effective because the players are more attentive and they get the message that defense is the most important part of the game. The coach who is organized develops teams that play with a purpose. Where disorganized teams with talent may be able to hold their own on offense, they will never reach their defensive potential and will often fall short of their expected goals. The organized coach prepares his team to succeed.

4. Be demanding.   Once the plan is in place, it is up to the coach to keep everybody on track. A constant effort, both physical and mental, is necessary to learn the defensive system in a progressive manner. Pay attention to even the slightest detail. Any mistakes that are made must be corrected immediately and not allowed to continue. This is best done by stopping the action, demanding eye-contact from all the players, correcting the mistake, then repeating the action until the coach's standards are met. Demand intensity in practice because effort in games reflects energy in practices. This effort can be affected by poor physical condition, so players must be in top shape to make the system work.

5. Be positive.   The coach has to believe in the defensive system and its opportunities for success before he can expect his players to follow along. Only when the players see a confident coach committed to teaching all facets of the defense does this system have a chance to work. Teach by positive reinforcement. While it is important to point out player mistakes, it is just as important to note and compliment proper executions. Enthusiasm enhances this positive approach and is often transferred into the team effort.

6. Be patient.   Patience is more than a virtue—it is a must. The team man-to-man defense takes a long time to teach, and it must be done in a step-by-step method. It will be necessary to review fundamentals every day of the year, and this can become tedious for both the players and coaches. These fundamentals, however, will eventually become habit—along with winning seasons for the patient, yet persistent, coach.

THE PLAYERS' ROLE

Along with a commitment on behalf of the coach, the success of the team man-to-man defense relies on the ability and the attitude of the players. We have found that players can be better on defense than they are on offense because less "fine-tuned" skills are needed. It is attitude that sets the limits on the effectiveness of defensive play. To make this team defense work, individual players must possess ample quantities of desire and determination: desire to be a good defensive player and determination to stop the other team from scoring. We want players motivated by the challenge of man-to-man defense who get upset when the other team scores. Our players must be aggressive and willing to hustle all over the court, taking the charge if necessary, diving for a loose ball, or doing anything that will help the defense to work. This defense depends upon a team effort, so individuals involved must pool their talents for the goal of stopping the other team.

THE RESULT

As the coaching scheme progresses and the team concept is introduced, the players develop a sense of confidence in the defense and in each other. This confidence carries over to the other end of the court, helping to instill the team concept into the entire program. What results is a team that plays with pride. This is indeed a team that is hard to beat. The word *pride* is over used and seldom understood, so we have spelled out to our players what it means to our program.

P—Practice. Give 100 percent in practice, 100 percent of the time.

R—Rules. Follow the playing rules on the court and the training rules off the court.

I—Individual. It is up to each individual to carry his weight to help the team succeed.

D—Defense.   The most important part of the game is defense.

E—Ego.   We must have a team ego; there is no room for individual egos.

What now follows in the upcoming chapters is a thorough look at a defensive system that has worked well for us at Concord High. The principles of the team man-to-man are discussed, with the fundamentals of the defense broken down in the manner in which they are taught to our players.

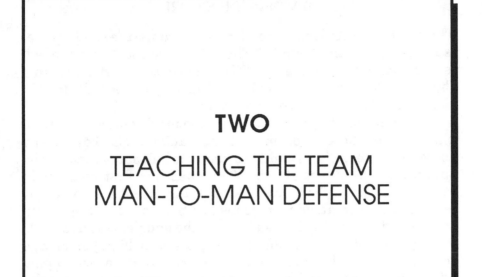

TWO

TEACHING THE TEAM MAN-TO-MAN DEFENSE

The team man-to-man defensive system incorporates man-to-man skills and positioning, and its aggressive nature is supported by zone concepts off the ball. The position of the defense is always determined by the location of the ball. Any time the ball moves, all defenders must move to maintain proper position. In explaining positioning to our players, we have divided the court into three sections as shown by Diagram 2-1.

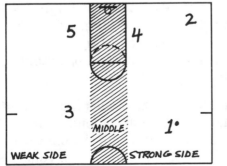

B - BALLHANDLER
P - POST
F - FORWARD
W - WING
WG - WEAK SIDE GUARD
WF - WEAK SIDE FORWARD

Diagram 2-1

DIVIDING THE COURT

The width of the foul lane extended to half-court (the shaded area) is referred to as the "middle." The side of the court that the ball is on is called the "strong side." The side of the court away from the ball is defined as the "weak side." As long as the ball stays in the middle, there is no strong or weak side.

We have built this defense from the inside out, and then we play it from the outside in. Let me explain. The key to any successful defense is its ability to keep the ball out of the middle, specifically the 3-second area. This was our first concern in structuring this defense. All passes to the inside are denied by post defenders in an advantageous position supported by weak-side defenders who sag in assistance to the middle. We have made it very difficult for the offense to enter this high-percentage scoring area. At the same time we instruct our players to play aggressively on the ball when it is on the perimeter, and it is the movement of the ball that dictates all of our defensive shifts and rotations. This on-the-ball pressure gives the impression of a defense overly concerned with the outside shot, when in essence it is all part of a bigger plan to keep the ball out of the middle. The beauty of the team man-to-man defense is that it puts constant pressure on the ball while at the same time protecting the area inside that is so crucial to offensive success.

TALKING ON DEFENSE

One factor that will help make this defense work is the art of communication among the players. We have found that if we ask our players to say too much, they say nothing. After years of shortening defensive statements, we have come up with the following terminology that packages useful and pertinent information in concise statements.

"I've got ball" Any time the ballhandler eludes his man and is picked up by another defender, this new defender makes this call to indicate that: (1) he is now covering the man with the ball, and (2) this man is not his natural match-up. Teammates are alerted to the new alignment and made aware that the defender has left his original match-up.

"Piece"— We make this call whenever the ball is deflected by a defender to alert teammates to recover the ball.

"Pick"— A defender makes this call any time the man he is guarding attempts to screen a teammate's man.

"Switch"— This usually follows a "pick" call and designates a changing of men.

"Stay"— This is another finish to the "pick" call telling a teammate to stay with his own man.

"Help"— A call made any time you are guarding the man with the ball and he beats you on a drive to the basket.

"Deny"— Any time the man you are guarding picks up his dribble, this call is made to instruct teammates to overplay and look to steal a pass or force a 5-second count.

We feel comfortable that these seven statements "say it all" for our defensive effort. Not too long ago we demanded that our team adhere to the "Ten Command-ments," but we have since dropped three terms that we felt overstated the defense. Our players no longer call "shot" when an outside shot is taken or "ball" when the rebound is secured, because one of the basic rules of this defense is to see the ball at all times and these calls become unnecessary. We also had our players call out "weak side" every time they sagged to the middle to verify support to their strong side teammates, but we found this call to be unneeded as well. Now with less to say, our players say more, and communication between teammates has improved.

UNDERSTANDING THE DEFENSE

For the players to best understand this man-to-man defense with its team concepts, rules must be made for them to follow. These rules must be:

1. explained thoroughly, so they are fully understood by each player;
2. consistent, so they make sense to the players; and
3. few in number, so they can be mastered by all.

System of Eight Rules

Our teaching system consists of eight rules. We spend time during the first week of practice going over these rules with the players, giving them an idea of what the defense is all about. With the "big picture" in mind, the players respond better to learning the fundamentals that make up the team man-to-man defense. Our eight rules for successful defense are:

1. Stop the player with the ball.
2. Force the ball wide out of the middle.
3. Deny strong-side passes.
4. Sag to the middle on the weak side.
5. Deny/front all post players.
6. Switch on all screens, on or off the ball.
7. Rotate to stop penetrating move to the basket.
8. Box out and get the rebound.

Our players are constantly reminded of these rules and are held accountable for all eight responsibilities at all times. Failure in any one area will bring a stoppage of play and correction in practice, and a coach's reaction and possible substitution in a game. The players must realize that the success of this defense relies on the efforts of all five players to fulfill all of the defensive rules. It only takes one player to let down in any one area for the entire system to fail, so we are very particular in correcting every mistake.

Explanation of the Eight Rules

1. Stop the player with the ball.   Defense begins when we take a shot at the offensive end. Even as attempts are made for offensive rebounds, each player must develop an awareness of where his defensive assignment is. The defensive effort commences immediately when the ball comes into the possession of the opposition. Stopping the player with the ball is our number-one objective.

If an offensive player pushes the ball down the floor, his defender must be in position to stop his penetration once the ball enters the front court. If the defender gets caught behind in transition, another defender must step up, call out "I've got ball," and we will adjust accordingly. Our first defensive responsibility is to stop the ball to slow the offense and allow us to match up so that we can put all of our defensive rules into effect. (See Photo 1.)

Once we have matched up, this rule remains our priority. Any time the player with the ball shakes free from his defender, the nearest teammate to the ball moves to him to stop penetration and we will rotate and take our chances off the ball. Our goal at each match-up is to keep the ball on the perimeter, force the opponent to pick up his dribble, then step up with a "deny" call to force a possible turnover. For this defense to work, the players must realize that the most dangerous opponent is the one with the ball.

2. Force the ball wide out of the middle. We constantly stress to our players the importance of on-the-ball defense. Constant pressure on the ball will make it difficult for the offense to dictate the "pace and place" of the offensive pattern. On-the-ball defense starts with a commitment to get the ball out of the middle. Forcing the ball to either side will establish a strong side and weak side allowing the weak-side defenders to sag to the middle. This gives the defense a five-on-four or five-on-three player advantage and allows for even more aggressive defense on-the-ball.

To accomplish this objective, we have established specific guidelines that our players follow whenever they are guarding the ball on the perimeter. One thing we have taken into consideration while establishing these guidelines is that the player with the ball has an advantage over his defender. He knows which way he is going and the defensive player can only react to offensive movement. For us to expect our players to shut down every on-the-ball match-up would be unrealistic and unattainable, so

Photo 1
Our top priority is to stop the player with the ball.

we are satisfied with having our players influence the offense to an area advantageous to our defensive scheme.

(a) Ball is in the middle   (See Diagram 2-2.) When the ball is in the middle of the court, we feel that we are at a disadvantage defensively. The defensive player must square up to influence his opponent to make a decision to go left or right. Once this choice is made and the ball starts moving in either direction, the defender reacts by dropping the outside foot and then sliding and retreating in the same direction. We never want to allow penetration across the foul line and demand that our players react and slide quickly to force the ball wide of the lane where they will find help.

We used to tell our players to determine the direction of the offense by overplaying in the middle of the court. We found that this caused too many positive scoring opportunities because we were getting beat regularly through the foul line and our support system is vulnerable in that situation. We now let the offense choose the side of the court they wish to attack and then apply our "force the ball wide" rule when they start in either direction.

(b) Ball is wide above the foul line extended   (See Diagram 2-3.) When the ball is out of the middle, the offense no longer gets free choice. The defender now plays to force his opponent even wider. To do this, a proper defensive stance must be maintained that creates an angle of overplay with the foot closest to the middle of the court forward. This takes away one choice for the offensive man, and the defender can now expect his opponent to

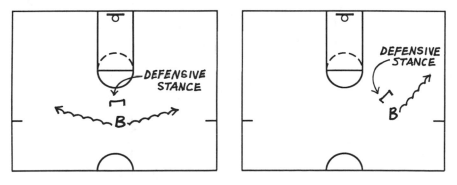

Diagram 2-2   Diagram 2-3

dribble toward the strong side which would be toward the rear foot in the defensive stance. We don't want to allow the offensive player a head start and constantly remind our players to react promptly to the initial offensive move and slide quickly to force the ball toward the sideline away from the basket. We now have a strong-side/weak-side situation with a support system that will strengthen as the ball moves wider and lower. Allowing the offensive man in this situation to dribble over the top of the defender to penetrate the middle is poorly defended by our rotation system and cannot be allowed to happen. (See Photo 2.) We tell our players that the only way the ball can move back to the middle is if the offense is willing to give up ground. If this should occur, the defender must square up to his man as soon as the ball enters the middle.

(c) Ball is wide below the foul line extended   (See Diagram 2-4.) Once the ball moves to the foul line extended, the defender must square his shoulders to the sideline to continue forcing the ball to the baseline. As before, our defense is equipped to support any penetration that is wide (in this case to the baseline side) and is vulnerable to any over-the-top middle penetration. If the defender is beaten to the basket, he calls "help," then runs as fast as he can in an attempt to re-establish good defensive position on his man. This calls for a sprint, not a defensive slide. If another teammate steps up to stop the ball before he can recover, he will then continue back to re-establish position on his own man, switch to his teammate's opponent, or trap—whatever the situation demands. The bottom line in this decision-making process is that

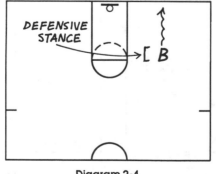

Diagram 2-4

Photo 2
Any time the dribbler attempts over-the-top penetration, the defender must move
his feet quickly to beat the ballhandler to a spot to force him to give up ground. We
can never allow penetration through the foul line.

stopping a drive to the basket is paramount because all the players know that the offensive man has a much better chance of scoring close to the basket than he has from the perimeter.

(d) Ball is wide in the baseline area (See Diagram 2-5.) Any time the ball is in the baseline area, we try to force the ball baseline into the teeth of this defense—our trap and rotation. Once again, over-the-top penetration weakens our rotation system while baseline penetration makes it work. When beaten, the defender runs alongside his man and then traps him when supported by the weak-side rotation. The offensive man is now "in jail" with his dribble used up and no open passing lanes due to our off-the-ball rotation system.

3. Deny strong side passes. Once the ball has been controlled and forced out of the middle, we must work to not allow passes to create opportunities for offensive penetration. Strong-side teammates are now a primary concern as they are only one pass away from the ball and become logical targets in the offensive process. Our players challenge all passes that we consider "penetrating passes"—passes that create an advantage for the offense. Strong-side players who are farther from the basket than the ball and are not considered in an advantageous position are not challenged. Their defenders sag toward the middle to better help support on-the-ball defense. Once again, the most dangerous offensive player is the one with the ball. Any time there is a "deny" call, every opponent is considered in an advantageous position

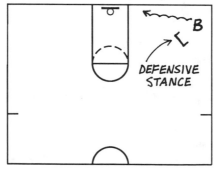

Diagram 2-5

because they will relieve pressure from the ballhandler, so our players must step up in the passing lanes to shut down all his options.

To effectively deny strong-side penetrating passes, a player must maintain a position between his man and the ball. This denial position, which is commonly referred to as "ball-you-man," calls for a balanced defensive stance with the inside foot up and the back to the ball. (See Diagram 2-6.)

The defender's inside hand is extended into the passing lane and the eyes are focused straight ahead, seeing both the man and the ball with peripheral vision. To get the ball, the offensive player must be forced to retreat from the basket toward the sideline to a position that no longer creates an advantage for the offense.

If this player goes backdoor, the defender pivots on his inside (back) foot and opens to the ball with the arms extended outward into the passing lanes. In this situation it is going to be impossible to see both man and ball, so we tell our players to see the ball and use both hands behind him to search for his opponent. The head is now on a swivel, looking at the ball, then quickly turning to locate the opponent. If the opponent is lost, reading the eyes of the player with the ball will help if he is loose in an advantageous position. We always want to know where the ball is; this is our primary concern in the team man-to-man defense.

We consider a backdoor cut a victory for defensive pressure. Offenses generally use this move as a secondary option, so we feel that we have taken our opponents out of their primary offensive

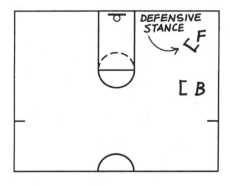

Diagram 2-6

pattern by forcing this backdoor cut. The sagging players from the weak side will help to defend this player once he reaches the middle of the court, so the backdoor cut is well defended in this defense.

4. Sag to the middle on the weak side.   Any time a defender is on the opposite side of the court than the ball is on, he sags to the middle to play support, or help, defense. This brings into our defense the zone concept of protecting the middle. It allows our players to play more aggressively on the ball and to front the low post without fear of getting beat for an easy basket.

Like all the other facets of the team man-to-man defense, weak-side defensive position is dependent upon location of the ball and position of the weak-side player, and any time either moves, the defender must move to maintain proper position.

(a) Defending the weak-side player above the foul line   We will allow the ball to enter the middle of the court or even reverse from side to side if the offense is willing to give up ground in the process. We do not contest nonpenetrating passes along the perimeter including guard-to-guard passes that reverse the strong side. We feel our players will easily adjust while the ball is in flight and no advantage is gained by the offense. Instead, we use our weak-side players to support the ball. If the weak-side player is above the foul line, his defender must move to a position where he has one foot over the midline of the court and is one step below the "line of the ball," an imaginary line from the weak-side player to the ball (see Diagram 2-7). Whenever the ball moves, the defender moves to maintain this position (see Diagram 2-8). This weak-side defender is ready to react in a multitude of ways. If the ball is dribbled "over the top," he must step up to stop penetration. If the defense succeeds to force baseline penetration, the weak-side guard must sprint to the basket to provide backside support. And finally, if the ball is passed to his man, he must react quickly to force his man wide to the strong side.

(b) Defending the weak-side player below the foul line   Many offenses utilize weak-side players by picking away for them or flashing them to the middle. This makes the positioning of weak-side defenders even more significant, since their men can readily

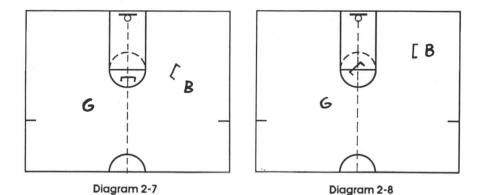

Diagram 2-7   Diagram 2-8

move to vulnerable inside areas. Providing support for ball penetration is still our primary weak-side objective, but we want our
players to be constantly aware of where their men are and
maintain proper positioning at all times. This positioning depends upon the location of the ball.

When the ball is above the foul line extended, the weak-side
defender below the foul line has one foot in the middle of the court
and the other on the weak side (see Diagram 2-9). He is one step
below the "line of the ball" and has an open stance with one arm
pointed toward his man and the other toward the ball. When the
ball or man moves, the defender moves as well to maintain this
ball-defender-man triangular relationship. We tell our weak-side
defenders that flat passes cannot be allowed to go through the
middle because they will shift the strong side too quickly for us
to move to areas to provide support to challenging the ball. Passes
to weak-side players must be forced to be lobbed over the defense
to give all defenders time to re-establish proper defensive position. We have found that our weak-side positioning has been
improved by having defenders in this area continuously point
with both arms—these "antennae" remind the brain where both
the man and ball are located.

When the ball goes below the foul line extended, the weak-
side defender moves to a point where he has both feet in the
middle, with the foot nearer the ball over the midline and on the
strong side of the court (see Diagram 2-10). He is still one step
below the "line of the ball" with an open stance, seeing and

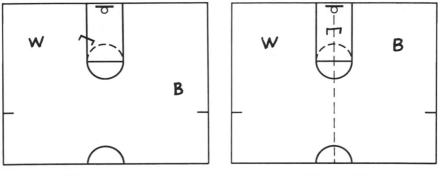

Diagram 2-9   Diagram 2-10

pointing to both his man and the ball. A cross-court pass is now more difficult for the offense, so this allows the weak-side defender to move further away from his man and into the middle. He is now a primary support man and must move to protect the basket any time there is strong-side penetration. The weak-side defender is also aware that his man might flash to the ball at any time and he is ready to quickly adjust to prevent his man from coming between him and the ball. Post defense begins when the weak-side player enters the middle. The weak-side defender will gain control of this man if he can beat him to a spot and force him to change his direction.

5. Deny/front all post players.   In order to be successful, the defense must keep the ball out of the middle. No penetrating dribble or pass to this area of the court can be allowed. It stands to reason, then, that we consider offensive players in the post area of vital importance and must constantly work to deny them the ball.

Keeping the ball out of the post area is an important part of any defensive scheme, yet a difficult task for any one player to accomplish. Post defense must be a team effort, and we have made it one of the central themes of our team man-to-man system. Post defense begins with constant pressure on the ball on the perimeter. This pressure makes it difficult for the ballhandler to sight open teammates inside and restricts the passing lane to any post player. Forcing the ball wide is also a significant part of post play. This establishes a strong side/weak side and allows weak-side players to sag to the middle to provide backside support to post coverage. The best passing angle to the post area comes from the corner, but our defense denies access to this area by denying strong-side passes and forcing forwards to go backdoor or wider to the sideline to receive the ball. With all defenders carrying out their responsibilities, denying the post is now a task that can be successfully accomplished.

To best teach post defense to our players, we have broken down the inside area into three sections: the low post, medium post, and high post (see Diagram 2-11). Defensive positioning on all post players will depend on which post position the offensive player is occupying and the location of the ball.

(a) Defending the low post   Most teams that we play against run an offense that is designed to get the ball into the low post. We feel that the low block is the most critical post area because of its proximity to the basket, and we spend time preparing all of our players to defend this position.

The low post always represents a penetrating pass, so constant attention must be given to any offensive player who occupies this space. Defensive positioning in this area will be determined by the location of the ball. Any time the ball is above the foul line extended, we play half a man around the low post in a denial position (see Diagram 2-12). Good on-the-ball defense combined with ball-you-man denial in the pivot will make the low block entry pass near impossible. When the ball moves below the foul

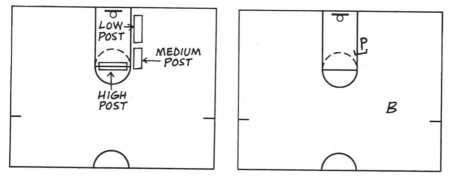

Diagram 2-11   Diagram 2-12

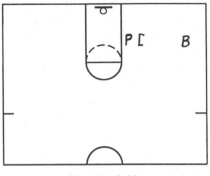

Diagram 2-13

line extended, the passing angle to the post improves dramatically, as does our defensive pressure. We now have our players front the low post (see Diagram 2-13) to force the offense to throw a lob pass against our on-the-ball pressure, over the post defender, and short of the weak-side support.

In the event that the ball does get into the low post area or into the middle close to the basket, the defender takes his position directly behind his man and holds his ground with his arms and hands straight up. (See Photo 3.) The defender cannot go for fakes and must maintain his verticality throughout this defensive effort. All other defenders will collapse to the middle to help and try to flush the ball back outside.

One of the keys to effective post defense is establishing defensive position before the offense is ready to pass the ball inside.

For example, on a strong-side pass that penetrates the foul line extended, the low post defender must be moving to front the post man while the ball is in the air. Waiting for the ball to be caught before adjusting defensive position would leave the post open for a quick pass to the baseline side and would also leave the post defender vulnerable to getting pinned by an alert post player.

(b) Defending the medium post Opponents sometimes position or flash players to the medium post area, so we must concern ourselves with defending this area of the lane as well. Medium post players are defended by a denial stance where the

Photo 3
When defending a low post player with the ball, maintain position with the feet and
keep the hands straight up.

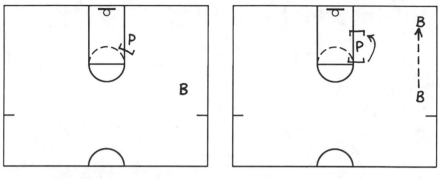

Diagram 2-14   Diagram 2-15

defender assumes a ball-you-man position and plays half a man around on the ballside (see Diagram 2-14).

His hand closer to the ball is extended to discourage the pass inside, and the hand away from the ball rests on the opponent's jersey to help monitor movement. If the ball should move to a position below the player, the defender must cross in front of his man ("come over the top") to a position below the opponent that will allow him to continue to discourage the post and also prepare him to help if the ball should penetrate the baseline (see Diagram 2-15).

We don't front the medium post. This player is too far away from the hoop, and we would be susceptible to lob passes for easy baskets even with the weak-side support. If the ball should get into the medium post, the defender assumes an on-the-ball defensive stance and attempts to force the ball wide. Back-to-the-basket moves are generally ineffective from this distance, so there is no need to play with the hands raised high unless the player uses up his dribble.

(c) Defending the high post   If there is an opponent stationed in the high post, the defender plays up a quarter man on the side of the ball to discourage the entry pass to this area. This is a difficult task when the ball is in the middle of the court and provides another reason why forcing the ball wide is important in our team defensive concept. If the ball is reversed from guard to guard (see Diagram 2-16), the high post defender goes behind

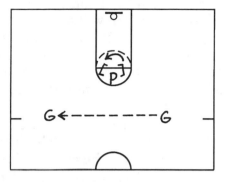

Diagram 2-16

his man. This is to prevent him from pinning the defender and then rolling and establishing good inside position.

Just as with medium post defense, the hand closer to the ball is extended to cut down the passing lane and deflect passes that are attempted. The hand away from the ball rests on the opponent's back. If the ball should get into the high post, the defender must immediately square up to his opponent and prevent any further penetration toward the basket. We are also aware that a high post player can easily become a medium or low post player, so whenever the ball crosses the foul line extended we must step to the ball and be ready to fight for defensive position along the lane.

6. Switch on all screens on or off the ball. To best maintain constant pressure on the ball and to keep defenders in position to deny penetrating passes, we have found that switching is the most effective way to deal with offensive screens. This puts maximum pressure on the player being screened for (the first option), and forces the offense to go to not-as-familiar second or third options. Continual switching also helps to keep our big men near the basket in good post and rebounding position and our guards on the perimeter where our defense operates most efficiently.

Communication is the key to make this facet of the defense work. If one defender feels that a switch is warranted, he must relate that to his teammate so that necessary adjustments can be made. We tell the defender of the screener to call out "pick" as soon as he realizes the intent of his man. Any further information, like "pick right" or "pick left" to an on-the-ball defender, or "pick coming" to a weak-side defender, will serve to increase the awareness of the situation and the efficiency of the defensive reaction. The "pick" call by itself is an incomplete call and must be finished with either a "switch" or "stay" call. On successful screens where contact is made between the screener and defender, we switch; but when there is no contact on the screen we stay with our men. If there is a question of whether to call "switch" or "stay," we tell our players to call and carry out a "switch." The defender being screened can also call "switch" if he cannot effectively stay with his man. Any time either player calls "switch," that becomes the dominant call and both players involved must immediately switch men.

(a) Screens off the ball   The two screens that we see most often off the ball are weak-side exchanges to occupy the help defense and screens that go away from the ball to free up weak-side players cutting to the middle. Both of these situations are best defended by the switching defense.

A team will weak-side exchange to keep weak-side defenders from sagging and to help bring the defensive forward out away from the basket. A switch on this screen will keep the guard out front to deny a quick reversal pass to the forward coming high and will leave the defensive forward low to help prevent ball penetration into the post area (see Diagram 2-17). Teams can weak-side exchange all they want: our guard will keep forcing the offensive player coming high farther away from the basket to get the ball and our forward will remain low in the middle of the court

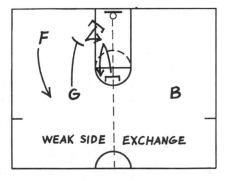

Diagram 2-17

where he can support on-the-ball pressure. No advantage is gained by the offense.

Many offenses run screens away from the ball to free up weak-side cutters moving toward the ball. This deals with the middle of the court so it becomes a major concern to our defense. To begin with, many of these screens are avoided by our weak-side defenders who sag off their men and have time to step around these stationary players before their men reach the middle. For those screens that are successful, we switch to take away the passing lane to the cutter. The screener's defender calls "pick!" then "switch!" and steps up to deny the pass inside (see Diagram 2-18). The screener now becomes a viable option, so the defender getting picked must fight to get around the screener to take away this secondary option. This, combined with good on-the-ball pressure, makes these inside passes low percentage ones for the offense.

(b) Screens on the ball The player with the ball is the most dangerous player on the court. We must do all that we can to prevent him from taking a wide open outside shot or from driving to the hoop. We switch on all on-the-ball screens to meet this objective and to force the offense away from shots they are used to taking. Once again, communication is important so that both defenders can switch immediately on contact, one defender jump switching onto the ball to continue to force it wide and the other defender fighting for inside position to take away movement toward the basket (see Diagram 2-19).

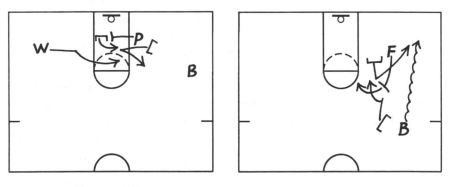

Diagram 2-18   Diagram 2-19

Many coaches are afraid to switch because of the possibility that the offense may "pick and roll" for an easy basket. This is admittedly one of the best plays in basketball, but my observations over the years lead me to believe that not many teams use it at all and very few use it effectively. At best it will work only occasionally, and teams certainly are not going to beat us with the "pick and roll." The on-the-ball defense and sagging weak side help to force a perfect pass to the player rolling to the basket, even if he gets his defender on his back. Perfect passes aren't thrown every time down the court. Constantly switching works for us because we feel that we gain a lot more by keeping continuous pressure on the ball than we lose by occasional "pick and roll" baskets.

With our team man-to-man concepts we are not concerned with mismatches that may result from switching. All of our players are schooled in each aspect of the defense, and we have confidence that they all can carry out their responsibilities. Switching may lead to minor adjustments, such as bigger players backing off quicker guards half a step or extra weak-side help for smaller players caught inside. Nonetheless, the rules remain in place and the aggressive on-the-ball defense continues with support from the weak side. Our goal is continuous pressure on the ball, and a switching man-to-man defense gets this done best.

7. Rotate to stop penetrating move to the basket.   It is unrealistic to believe that we could teach all of our players to shut down the ball every time it came into the possession of the man they are guarding. Experience has taught us that we would be more successful influencing the ball in one direction or the other and using defenders off the ball to support ball penetration to the middle. This philosophy has formed the framework of the team man-to-man defensive system.

We funnel the ball wide and force dribble penetration along the baseline because, with the weak-side rules we have established, this offensive move will result in a defensive advantage. Any dribble on the baseline triggers a rotation in which the weak-side forward's defender sprints to the ball in an effort to stop penetration before it reaches the lane. The man on the ball rides the inside shoulder to keep his man along the baseline and

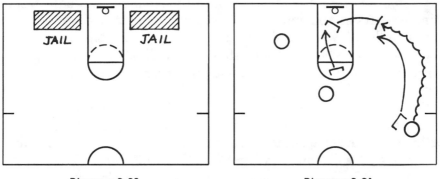

Diagram 2-20   Diagram 2-21

then traps with the weak-side forward's defender just before the lane is reached by the dribbler. The offensive man is now in "jail" (see Diagram 2-20). With the weak-side guard's defender rotating down, all dangerous passing lanes are shut down (see Diagram 2-21).

Five Keys to Making This Rotation Work

(a) Timing   Players must rotate simultaneously to put maximum pressure on the ball while not exposing their men prematurely. Our rule is simple: when the ball is dribbled toward the basket in the baseline area, we rotate. We have found that any movement before the dribble opens up passing lanes and breaks down the defense. As long as the ball is being held in this area, we maintain our deny, strong-side, and weak-side help positions. Once the ball leaves the hand for dribble penetration, all five defenders move. The weak-side forward's defender and the man on the ball put the ballhandler in jail, forcing him to pick up his dribble and set a 5-second count in motion. The post defender maintains a ball-you-man position with his man. The weak-side guard's defender sprints down to shut off the pass across the lane to the offensive forward. The strong-side guard's defender sags to the low post to help defend this area. Upon seeing the low post well guarded, the next move for this defender is to the middle to shut off a possible pass to the weak-side guard who will be somewhere around the foul line (see Diagram 2-22).

(b) Recovery   Ideally we would like to steal the ball every time we get our opponents in jail, but our concern with protecting the middle allows for the ball to be thrown out to the perimeter. We know that when we double-team the ball, we can't account for all four of the remaining offensive players, so we will give up the pass that will hurt us the least—the one away from the basket. When that pass is thrown, all five defenders must be on the move while the ball is in the air to gain advantageous positions on their men. The nearest defender to the player receiving the ball sprints to him and calls out "I've got ball!" if this isn't his natural match-up. If it is his own man, he says nothing. This conveys the message that he is on his original man. Other defenders go to the men nearest them with priority going to those closest to the ball and most logical to be passed to. The defender on the ball forces baseline, the defenders inside take away passing lanes to their men, weak-side defenders sag to help, and we try to put the ball in jail again. No opponents have perfect escape records from our jail.

(c) The low post remains covered at all times   Leaving this position uncovered during a defensive rotation would give the offense a simple and effective outlet that could lead to a high-percentage scoring attempt. We want the defender on the low post to maintain his position between his man and the ball throughout the baseline rotation. It is up to the low defender on the weak side to stop the ball before it reaches the lane (see Diagram 2-23).

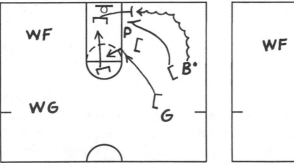

Diagram 2-22

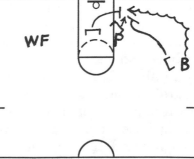

Diagram 2-23

There will be times when the defender on the low post will have to stop baseline penetration, and we must adjust our defense to these situations. They occur when the ball is penetrated directly at the low post or when the low post defender is pinned below his man when baseline penetration is taking place. In these two situations, the low post defender steps up to stop the dribble penetration and the low weak-side defender changes his route from the ball to the man on the low post. He will receive help in this area from the strong-side guard's defender whose initial responsibility is to sag to the low post area (see Diagram 2-24).

(d) The ball is forced wide and penetration is restricted to the baseline area Before we can have a successful rotation to the ball, two conditions must be met. First, the ball must be forced out of the middle to set up a strong side and weak side. This will help to define responsibilities for our players and put us in proper position to stop the ball from penetrating to the basket. Any penetration through the foul line is poorly resisted by our defenders who now must step up to stop the ball without guarantee of backside support on their men (see Diagram 2-25).

Forcing the ball wide is an important first step, but a successful rotation still relies on strong-side influence toward the baseline. Any dribble penetration over the top of the on-the-ball defender puts the entire defense at a disadvantage. Weak-side defenders must now move to stop the ball, leaving open passing angles to weak-side offensive teammates in good scoring position

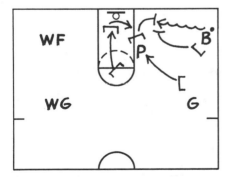

Diagram 2-24

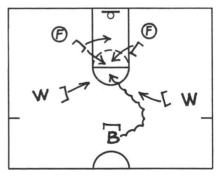

Diagram 2-25

(see Diagram 2-26). All defenders must realize that foul line and over-the-top penetration hurt the team man-to-man defense and they must work hard on the ball at all times not to let these situations occur.

(e) Properly adjusting when there are not two offensive players on the weak side   Most of the time, teams will balance the court with players on both the strong and weak sides. There will be times, however, when there will be fewer than two offensive players on the weak side, so our players must be constantly aware of offensive positioning to be able to quickly adjust to any unusual situation.

Some teams will "overload," putting four players on the same side of the court as the ball and leaving only one weak-side player. Any time the ball penetrates along the baseline, the low defender on the weak side moves to stop it before it reaches the lane. With only one player on the weak side, no matter where he is located, he is the low man and must stop the ball. The next nearest defender to the weak side (never the low post defender) sees three other teammates on the strong side and realizes that he must move to protect the low weak side. All other rotation responsibilities remain the same (see Diagram 2-27).

In cases where a team puts all five players on the same side of the court, we will drop the defender farthest from the ball (usually the point) into the lane to help support lob passes inside and baseline penetration (see Diagram 2-28). This gives us one

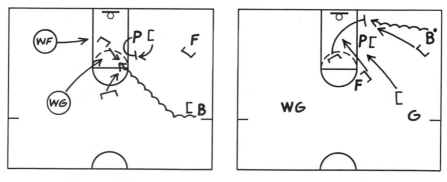

Diagram 2-26   Diagram 2-27

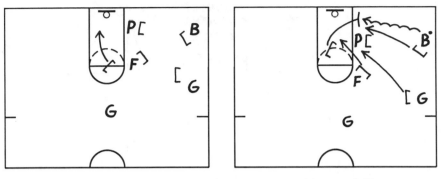

Diagram 2-28   Diagram 2-29

weak-side player and the ability to rotate to stop baseline pene-tration while providing backside support (see Diagram 2-29). Once again, this adjustment results from player understanding of the defense. Situations that call for slight deviations from our basic defensive rules must be drilled over and over again in practice.

8. Boxing out and getting the rebound. The defense works hard to force opponents to miss the shots they take. It would be counterproductive not to secure the rebounds. There is nothing more disheartening to the defensive effort than playing solid defense, forcing a contested outside shot, and then giving up an easy basket when the ball is rebounded by the offense. The defensive players must realize that their job isn't complete until the rebound is recovered.

The team man-to-man defensive system assigns defenders to certain offensive players. These defenders must move to help stop the ball, but ultimately they are responsible for boxing out their own men once a shot is taken. This being the case, we do not spend much time teaching our players *who* to box out, but rather on *how* to box out.

When a shot is attempted, offensive players are now consid-ered to be in one of two areas: the *box-out area* or the *check-and-go area* (Diagram 2-30). The box-out area is the space near the basket into which most of the rebounds fall. The check-and-go area is the section of the court farther away from the basket. On a shot,

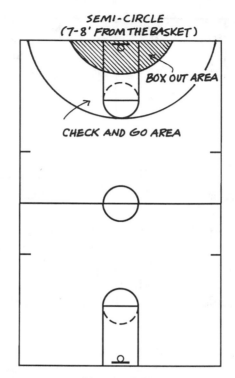

Diagram 2-30

players in the box-out area must first contact their men with their hands or arms, then pivot to make contact with the butt. This inside position should be held until the ball is located and the effort is made to retrieve it. Any ball that caroms within reach must be aggressively grabbed by both hands to insure control. We send all five players to the box-out area in an all-out effort to obtain every rebound. Defenders guarding players in the check-and-go area must first look to make contact with any opponent moving to the basket, then quickly turn and sprint to the box-out area ahead of this opponent to help rebound the ball. In the event that the opponent backs away and doesn't crash the boards, the defender still moves toward the basket to increase our chances of possession.

Most shots that are attempted from one side of the court will be rebounded on the other side. Our weak-side defenders must realize this and react to achieve good rebounding position. These defenders are at the midline of the court when a perimeter shot is taken, and movement straight to the hoop will allow their men to be in premium rebounding position on the weak side. The weak-side defender must be drilled to turn to find his man as soon as a shot is released and then move to a spot between his man and the basket where he can make contact to keep his man on his back (Diagram 2-31). Now facing the basket, he can find the ball and go after it.

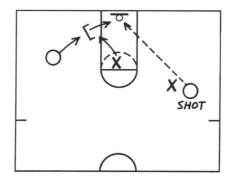

Diagram 2-31

A FINAL WORD

Developing an effective team man-to-man defense will take much time and effort, but implementing this system that doesn't allow easy inside baskets and forces the offense to play away from the basket along the perimeter will pay big dividends at the defensive end and may well be the reason for a winning program.

THREE

TEACHING THE FUNDAMENTALS OF THE TEAM MAN-TO-MAN DEFENSE

In order to effectively play the team man-to-man defense, a commitment must be made to work at it every day, all season long. Individual and team skills must be developed and reinforced from the first day of practice to the last. This is done in a systematic fashion where the fundamentals are thoroughly ingrained into each player so that all situations are met by proper, automatic responses.

PLAYER ATTITUDE

We have found that where athletic talent is certainly an asset to defensive ability, a player does not excel at the defensive end of the court unless he possesses the desire and determination to do so. Therefore, our primary concern in conveying defensive principles to the team is to have each individual develop within himself the desire to be a good defensive player. We want players who are personally challenged on defense and who get upset when the opposition scores. Our players must be fundamentally sound on defense, but also determined enough to stay low and move the feet constantly in an effort to outwork and subdue the offense.

This determination leads to the development of aggressiveness, which is a necessary prerequisite to effective defense. Teams cannot play good defense without being aggressive. We explain aggressiveness to our players as the attitude that we are going to control the offense by making them do what we want, not what they want, backed up by the effort to make this happen. Understanding defensive rules and developing individual fundamental skills is a means to this end, but our players must also possess the depth of determination that compels them to put forth the sustained effort necessary for these rules to work. This attitude is reflected every time a player takes a charge or dives on the floor after a loose ball. We feel that every loose ball is ours and this aggressive approach has gone a long way to making our defensive effort a successful one.

THE FUNDAMENTALS OF DEFENSE

Individual defensive techniques must be thoroughly learned before effective team pressure can be exerted. As in any defensive system, proper execution of individual fundamental skills is the foundation of the team man-to-man defense. We spend a lot of time in practice working on these skills in an attempt to build sound defensive habits that will allow our players to react intelligently to any situation they may face in a game. (See Photo 4.)

FUNDAMENTAL 1: ON-THE-BALL DEFENSE

All defensive teaching begins with developing the basic stance. (See Photo 5.) We spend a significant amount of time in the preseason working with our players to get them into a defensive position where they can move quickly in any direction. Our major concern in the team man-to-man defense is to stop the ball, so the most important fundamental that we teach is the one that serves to fulfill this objective.

Photo 4

Practice time spent on defense will pay big dividends for the team.

Photo 5
The basic defensive stance.

Defending the triple threat. The toughest player to guard is the one who has yet to use his dribble. (See Photo 6.) This player is a triple threat because he can shoot, pass, or dribble—and all of these options must be provided for by the defense. We want our defender to be close enough to his man so that he could reach out and touch him (2 feet–2½ feet). A greater distance alleviates the pressure we are trying to apply. Being too close puts the defender at risk of getting beat to the basket by a drive.

The feet must be slightly wider than the shoulders, with the inside foot up to force the ball wide and the toes of the outside foot even with the heel of the inside foot (toe-heel position). The knees are bent and the butt is down allowing the back to be at a 45-degree angle to the floor and the head to be up. With the weight

Photo 6
Defending an opponent in triple threat.

on the balls of the feet, the body is balanced, and is certainly a key to good defense. The head is up, with the chin off the chest, and is located above the midpoint of the feet. Both arms are extended with the outside (lead) arm bent at the elbow with the fingers pointing to the ball. If the offensive player brings the ball above his shoulders, the defensive player maintains his defensive stance and raises this arm to a position where he can contest a shot or overhead pass. The inside (back) arm is extended with the forearm parallel to the floor and the palm up in a position to close off the passing lane to the middle. If the offensive man lowers the ball below the waist as if to start a dribble, the lead arm drops and prepares to pressure the ball to help force the dribbler wide.

We react to all foot fakes, or jab steps, toward the basket with a quick shuffle back with both feet equal to the distance of the offensive stride. This maintains proper defensive distance so that if the offensive player now dribbles, the defender has allowed himself room to adjust to sustain advantageous defensive position. If the offensive player returns his foot to its original position, the defender steps up quickly to regain his defensive position an arm's length away from his opponent.

Our alignment on the offensive player varies with the location of the ball. The only time we line up toe-to-toe, face-to-face with our opponent is when the ball is located near the midline of the court. If the ball is being held in triple threat on one side of the court or the other, we line up on the inside shoulder to force any penetration toward the baseline and away from the middle.

Any time the offensive man attempts a shot, we want our players to bother the release. Uncontested shots reflect lack of pressure and cannot be allowed to happen in this defensive system. We react to the leap of the shooter by jumping straight up and extending an arm to the line of the ball. We have found that bothering the release in this manner is much more effective than attempting to limit the shooter's vision by putting a hand in his face. Our goal in defending the shooter is not to block shots. We are satisfied with forcing the shooter to adjust his release.

Defending the dribbler. Once the offensive man begins his dribble, the defender must stay low and wide to hold a quickness advantage over his opponent. (See Photo 7.) Both arms are now outside the knees, with the forearms parallel to the floor and the hands held with the palms up. The inside (back) hand is used to help force the offensive player to the outside. If the player is dribbling with his right hand, the defensive player's inside hand would be his right. The outside (or lead) hand digs at the ball in an attempt to poke it away or force the offensive player to pick up his dribble. We must constantly remind our players that this hand helps to control and bother the offensive player without reaching in.

Our alignment on the offensive player's inside shoulder forces him to the outside, or to the rear foot in the defensive stance. We tell our players that guarding the dribbler becomes a

Photo 7
Defending the dribbler.

series of three or four footraces where the player who gets to a spot first forces the other to alter his direction. We should expect the offensive player to move toward the outside, and when this occurs we must react quickly with our defensive slide to a spot that forces the offense even wider. Our lower center of gravity allows us to win every short race, and we feel that we can ride any offensive player away from the basket with proper execution of the defensive slide.

When performing a defensive slide, the player must keep a wide base and slide each foot about three inches. The weight is kept on the balls of the feet, and they are moved in such rapid fashion that they don't lift from the floor—they slide along it. Dribble defenders get in trouble when their feet come together and their ability to change direction is curtailed dramatically. We avoid this problem with our short strides. A proper stance and adept defensive slides will keep the defender's feet apart and will increase his quickness and balance. It allows each one of our players to control the direction of the ball and will often force the offense to pick up the dribble away from the basket.

On those occasions when the defender is beaten on a drive, he should turn and sprint in an attempt to regain defensive position. In the likely event that a teammate rotates to pick up his man before he can recover, the defender then must take his teammate's opponent or double-team his man, depending on the location of the ball.

Defending the discontinued dribble.   When a player picks up his dribble, the defender steps up and attacks the ball. (See Photo 8.) In assuming this "belly-to-belly" position, the defensive player maintains a toe-heel base along with a slight knee flex. We don't leave our feet until the offensive player does, and we block any pivot toward daylight with our wide base and quick feet. The arms are fully extended, and the hands mirror the ball in an attempt to get a piece of any pass to force a turnover. We must be careful not to let the offensive player off the hook by reaching in and fouling him. The defender yells, "deny, deny, deny, . . ." to alert teammates to move into passing lanes in a total effort to shut off passing options. A real key to the success of the deny position is a quick reaction by the defender once the dribbler is picked up. Immediate pressure on a discontinued dribble is an effective defensive strategy.

On-the-ball defense consists of these three phases. Our players will have success if they develop a proper stance that allows for the quickness they need, learn to read tendencies of offensive players, and work to make instant transitions from one phase to another. We want all of our players to have the attitude that they can stop anybody on defense. With proper conditioning, both physical and mental, players will develop the stamina, intelligence, and confidence needed to support this desire to dominate the offense. We have found that this is best accomplished with daily drills that force the players to concentrate on the fundamental aspects of the defense.

Drills to Improve On-the-Ball Defense

Stance drill.   Teaches the basic man-to-man techniques. This drill is used primarily as a preseason drill, but can be used on occasion throughout the season to review proper defensive mechanics.

Photo 8
Defending the discontinued dribble.

Phase 1: See Diagram 3-1. Players line up facing the base-line all with a line of vision to the coach. After describing and demonstrating the essentials of proper defensive stance, the coach commands his players to get into a defensive stance. This is done by the coach calling out "Stance!" The players react by slapping the floor with both palms, yelling "Defense!" and getting into proper defensive position with an imaginary man an arm's length away.

Early in the season we have the players hold this position while the coach goes around to correct poor stances. The team will stay in their stance anywhere from 45 seconds to a minute before

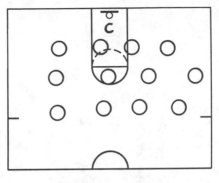

Diagram 3-1

the coach says, "Everybody up," and this is met by clapping and cheers of encouragement from a team excited to play defense. We will repeat this phase of the drill two or three times to work on form, knowing that at the same time the legs are being conditioned to increase stance stamina and the mind is being conditioned to understand this most important fundamental skill.

Emphasize: Proper stance; be fanatical about every detail.

Phase 2: The coach next explains to the players how to execute the most effective defensive slide. We stress quick feet with short strides and forbid long, loping slides that bring the feet together. Longer strides can generate more speed, but we want our players to realize that defense is best played with quickness. Short strides are much more effective than long ones.

The players are reminded that the first step in a defensive slide should always be made with the foot nearest the direction he wants to go. This lead foot should open as it strides to point in the direction the body is moving. This will allow the player to better slide along the floor.

After sufficient description and demonstration, the drill starts from the beginning. The coach yells "Stance!" and the players react by hitting the floor, yelling "Defense!" and getting into their stance. They hold this position for about 15 seconds while the coach reminds them that proper stance is important in building a positive attitude toward defense within each player.

The coach then starts phase 2 of this drill by saying "Here we go" and pointing to the left or right. The players then defensive slide in that direction and switch direction every time the coach points the other way. The players slide for at least 30 seconds before the coach says, "Everybody up" and is met with cheers and shouts of enthusiasm from a team excited to play defense.

Emphasize: Quick shuffle movement, stance, feet apart, head up, arms out, palms up.

Phase 3: In the final phase of this drill, the coach starts by instructing his players how to force a ballhandler right and left. Our defensive system relies on our ability to force the ball wide, so this is an important lesson for our players to learn. The players are told that in order to force the ball right, the right foot must be forward and the head must be lined up with the offensive player's left shoulder. Forcing left calls for the left foot to be forward and alignment to be on the right shoulder. Jab steps must be reacted to by quick shuffle steps to maintain proper distance. Any dribble penetration must be forced wide, and this is done by defensive sliding at an angle that will ride the offensive player to the sideline. After sufficient explanation and demonstration, the drill starts over from the beginning.

The coach calls for "Stance!" and phase 1 and phase 2 go on as before. After about 15 seconds of lateral slides, the coach yells, "Stop!" The players stop in their tracks and stay in their defensive stances. The coach then orders, "Force me right!" and the players react by moving both feet in a quick jump to proper position with the right foot forward. The players all yell "Right!" as they are moving. We want our players to be able to think and talk at the same time.

A jab step by the coach may follow, and all players react by moving both feet back slightly to maintain their arm's length distance. If the coach raises the ball above his shoulder, the players react by raising a hand to counter this move. The coach then commands, "Force me left!" and the players jump to proper position and yell "Left!" More fakes and reactions follow.

The coach then dribbles at his players (see Diagram 3-2), and they respond by sliding at an angle to force the ball wide and

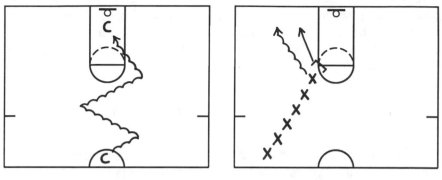

Diagram 3-2   Diagram 3-3

calling out the direction ("Left!"). When the ball changes direction, the players push off their opposite foot to stay with the ball and the new direction is called out ("Right!"). The players go back and forth down the court until the coach picks up his dribble and hears his players yell, "deny, deny, deny, . . ." and wave their arms to shut down the discontinued dribbler. The ball is thrown into the sea of arms and the player who steals it is greeted with enthusiasm by the rest of the players. We must stay excited to play defense.

The players then turn and repeat the entire process back up the court.

Emphasize: Stay low, head up, react to offensive movement, quick transition from triple threat to dribble to deny, enthusiasm.

Elbow drill.   Teaches stance; on-the-ball rules.

See Diagram 3-3. The players line up at the elbow of the foul lane with the first player in line the defender and the next player the ballhandler. The defender hands the ball to the ballhandler and immediately assumes a defensive stance that will limit passing and shooting ability (an arm's length away) and that will force the ballhandler to dribble wide to penetrate. By starting at the elbow and out of the middle, the defender knows he must contain his man to this side of the court. The only condition that allows a dribble toward the middle is if the ballhandler gave up ground to the basket to do so.

The defender lines up on the ballhandler's inside shoulder. His inside foot is up and wide of the offensive man's feet to insure penetration to the outside. Any penetration attempted to the inside should result in an offensive foul. As the ballhandler starts his drive to the outside, the defender must react immediately to ride him wide to the sideline. Giving the offensive player a head start in this drill will result in an easy basket. We tell our players, however, that any mistakes that result in penetration to the outside will still be supported by weak-side help. Mistakes that allow inside penetration (especially across the foul line), are unsupported and unforgivable. Therefore, we tell our players not to overreact to fakes wide leaving them susceptible to inside drives and not to lunge with their defensive slides allowing the offense to reverse dribble into the middle after starting a drive wide. We must always be conscious of pushing the ball wide.

The play continues until the defender secures the ball (on a steal or rebound), the ball goes out of bounds, or the ballhandler scores. The defensive player then goes to the end of the line and the offensive player becomes the defender against a fresh team- mate.

Emphasize: Quick transitions, stay low and quick, never allow middle penetration, beaten by outside penetration still allows us weak-side help opportunities.

Force wide drill.   Teaches techniques necessary to force the ball out of the middle; conditioning.

See Diagram 3-4. A defender (X) is selected to challenge a ballhandler (B1) who is in the middle of the court above the top of the key. Two more players, or wings (O1 and O2), are stationed at the foul line extended ready to receive a pass from the ballhandler. Another ballhandler (B2) awaits in the half-court circle to receive a pass from the wing to keep constant pressure on the defender.

The coach starts the action of the drill with a whistle. The ballhandler attempts to beat the defender through the foul line while the defender stays low and uses his wide base and quick feet to force the dribbler wide. With the ball in the center of the court, the defender must square up to the ballhandler until he

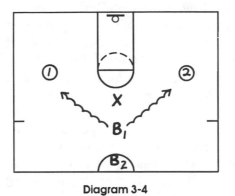

Diagram 3-4

chooses a direction. Once the ball starts moving toward a side, the defender steps up slightly with the inside foot to influence the dribbler to keep going wide. In this drill, the ball is dribbled until it passes the foul line or foul line extended, when it is then passed to the wing on that side. The wing passes the ball out to a fresh ballhandler in the center circle who starts his attempt at dribbling the ball across the foul line. The defender releases his man as soon as the ball crosses the foul line and sprints toward half-court to pick up his next assignment. He must come under control as he approaches the dribbler and get low and wide to force this player outside of the foul line as well. We continue this process for 45 seconds, when a whistle sounds and the team cheers the effort of a tired defender. This defender and one of the ballhandlers move to wing, the other ballhandler becomes the defender, and two fresh ballhandlers move to the midcourt area.

Emphasize: Force the ball wide of the foul line, stay low, keep moving the feet, "dig deep" for 45 seconds of effort.

Stop-the-drive drill. This drill teaches players how to attack a dribbler and force him wide.

See Diagram 3-5. The coach has the ball and passes to the offensive player located on the side below the foul line. The defensive player must start with one foot in the three-second area and move on the pass to stop the offensive player's drive to the basket. Often, in our defensive system, a player must sag off his

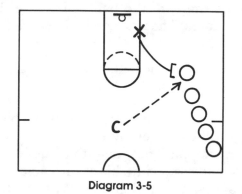

Diagram 3-5

man to help in the middle. Once the ball is passed to his man, he must move while the ball is in the air to establish a position that will force the ball wide. This drill addresses this situation.

In this drill, the offensive man must drive to the middle. Forcing him baseline is a victory for the defense. Allowing the offensive player to penetrate over the top of the defender cannot be allowed as our support system for this type of drive is weak. Any offensive movement in this direction must be forced away from the basket. By our rules, we want to ride the man wide toward the baseline, force him to pick up his dribble, and then step up with both arms extended hollering "Deny, deny, deny..." (See Diagram 3-5a.) Whenever a shot is attempted, the defender must first box out and then go get the ball. Play continues until

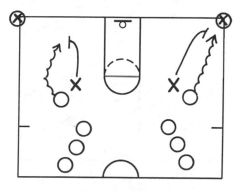

Diagram 3-5a

the defender gets the ball, the ball goes out of bounds, or the offensive player scores. The rotation is then offense to defense to the end of the line.

Emphasize: Attack the ball under control, force toward the baseline.

Zigzag drill. This drill teaches turning the dribbler.

See Diagram 3-6. Players line up on the baseline with the first two players stepping out, one a defender and the other a dribbler. The defender gets into his stance an arm's length away from the ballhandler in an alignment to force him one way or another. On the dribble, the defender uses quick, lateral slides to beat the offensive player to a spot, steps up as if to take a charge, and forces his man to reverse dribble and change direction. He

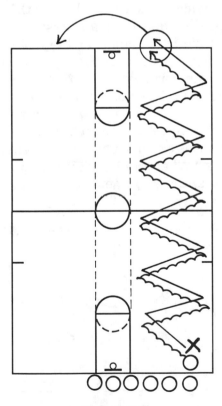

Diagram 3-6

then reacts to this dribble reversal by sliding in the opposite direction in order to beat the dribbler to another spot to once again make him turn. This action continues down the court until the ball reaches the opposite baseline. The players then switch roles and move to the other side of the court where they return with the defender turning the dribbler as many times as he can. To confine the offense and eliminate any chance of collision, the dribbler is limited by the sideline and an imaginary line that keeps the ball out of the middle of the court.

Players must constantly be reminded to keep their feet apart so that reactions to reverse dribbles are instantaneous. This can be accomplished only with short, quick slides. Long defensive slides bring the feet together and lead to careless transitions from one direction to the other, allowing the offensive player a head start on every turn. It is essential to maintain proper defensive position on each turn. This is done with a drop step by the inside foot and a simultaneous push off the outside foot to pursue a new angle to beat the dribbler to yet another spot on the floor to turn him again. Proper defensive fundamentals must be stressed in every drill to ensure that each player will gain the know-how and ability to control the offensive player.

It is important to point out to the players that although this drill is set up in a full-court format, it is designed to improve half-court defensive skills. The turning technique that is being addressed here is used to keep the ball on the strong side of the court. We want to discourage dribble penetration over the top of the defender to the middle and find that turning the player back toward the baseline helps to make the defensive system work.

This drill works best with three basketballs and players waiting until the group in front of them is at half-court before starting. The short rest in between provides recovery time for the players and allows them to go full steam down the court each time.

Early in the season we have our players do this drill with their hands behind their backs to stress footwork. Next, we bring the hands into play but don't allow them to reach to poke the ball away. When we feel comfortable with their defensive slides, we introduce the importance of the hands in guarding the dribbler. Players must use the hands to apply constant pressure on the ball. Keeping the hands in palm-up position, the defender pressures the ball with the hand nearer the direction of the dribble. Any crossover dribble in front of the body must be denied with the hands to prevent the offensive player from changing directions too quickly. Occasionally we vary this drill by telling the offensive players not to turn and having the defender pick up as many charges as he can down the floor. Another variation is to play live past half-court where the offense tries to beat the defense for a basket.

Emphasize: Quick reactions (No head starts!), beat the man to a spot, dominate the offense.

Deflect-the-pass drill.   Teaches pass recognition and anticipation.
See Diagram 3-7. Players spread out in groups of threes with each group having two passers about 15 feet apart and one defender in between them. The action resembles "monkey in the middle," with the defender attacking the player with the ball ready to deflect any pass thrown to the other offensive player. No lob passes are allowed and the player with the ball may dribble one time to force the defender to adjust his line of attack. Action continues for 45 seconds after which the whistle blows and a new defender moves to the middle.

Adding the dribble to this drill helped us to better simulate game conditions. How a defender attacks a player in triple threat position is different than how he attacks a player on the move, or a player who has used up his dribble. Allowing this dribble has forced the defender to be aware of the situation and to react

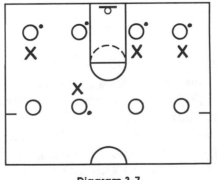

Diagram 3-7

accordingly. Against a player in triple threat, he moves quickly, yet under control, ready to defend a shot, pass, or dribble (a dribble or pass in this drill). Against the dribbler, he moves to beat the player to a spot to force him in the direction that would best suit our defense. Hands come up as the ball is picked up to shut down passing lanes. Against the player who has used up his dribble, the attack is all out in "Deny, deny, deny . . . " fashion. The hands are up and active, knowing that the offensive player must remain stationary and a pass is his only option.

Emphasize: Move while the ball is in the air, don't overreact to fakes, get a "piece" of the ball.

Defend-the-shooter drill.   Teaches techniques necessary to defend the shooter.

See Diagram 3-8. The defender hands the ball to the offensive player and gets into a defensive position appropriate to his location on the floor. The offensive player has the option of shooting immediately or taking one or two dribbles to set up his shot. The defender then must defend the triple threat position, react to the dribble, rise to contest the shot, then box out and get the ball. Play continues until the offense scores or the defense gets the ball. Once again we rotate from offense to defense to the end of the line.

Throughout this drill we are constantly reminding our players of the rules on contesting shots. First, the offensive man must leave the floor before the defender does—we cannot overreact to

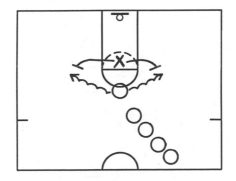

Diagram 3-8

shot fakes. Second, we are going to challenge all shots with the opposite hand. If the shooter is right handed, we are going to extend our left hand to bother the release. This will allow us to go straight up and avoid turning our bodies and getting ourselves off balance and unable to box out. Finally, as soon as the ball is released, we want our players to think rebound. The defender must make contact with the shooter, even if he is on the perimeter, and then move to the ball to be part of the rebounding action.

Emphasize: Go straight up, no fouls, box out and get the ball.

Loose-ball drill.   Teaches going after loose balls, one-on-one defense.

See Diagram 3-9. This drill begins with two lines on the baseline with the first player in each line just wide of the foul lane. The coach stands under the basket and rolls the ball slowly straight up the middle of the floor. On his whistle, the first player in each line sprints out and attempts to recover the loose ball. The player who comes up with possession is on offense, and the other player becomes the defender. The two players then go one-on-one to the basket with the play ending when the defender secures the ball, the ball is forced out-of-bounds, or the offense scores.

This drill is good at promoting the aggressive attitude that is needed to make this defensive system work. Players must go on the floor to get the ball. Floorburns are a necessary part of the good defensive player's uniform.

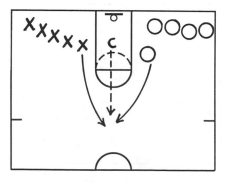

Diagram 3-9

Emphasize: Get the ball! If unsuccessful, react quickly to a defensive position.

Conditioning Drills Involving Defensive Stance

Reaction drill.   Teaches stance, reaction, and conditioning.

See Diagram 3-10. Players form four lines on the baseline with the coach out beyond half-court. On the whistle, the players at the front of each line sprint to half-court, slap their hands on the midcourt line, yell "Defense!" and run in place in rapid-fire style. This calls for the players to be in proper defensive stance, with the head up, knees bent, and base wide, with the weight on the balls of the feet. The feet move up and down, not more than an inch off the floor in a rapid fire manner. Over a period of time this will help condition the legs to improve stance stamina.

When the coach points, the players quickly get into a natural defensive stance and slide diagonally back to the baseline, changing direction when directed by the coach. As the players near the baseline, the coach raises both hands to signal the players to sprint forward to the foul line and run in place using rapid-fire technique (Diagram 3-11).

When the coach now points, the players once again get into natural defensive stances and laterally slide back and forth across the court. On the whistle, these four players sprint to the opposite end of the court, touch the baseline, and sprint back to conclude

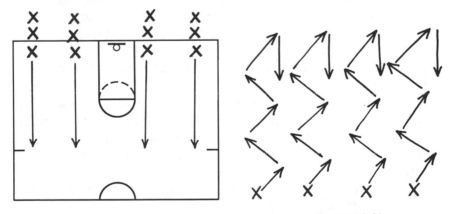

Diagram 3-10   Diagram 3-11

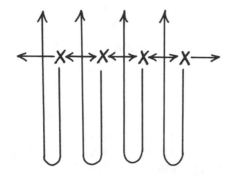

Diagram 3-12

their segment of the drill (Diagram 3-12). Simultaneously (using the same whistle as their signal), the next four players sprint to midcourt to begin the drill.

Emphasize: Keep the feet apart, get the feet off the floor in rapid fire, 100 percent effort—100 percent of the time.

Agility drill. Teaches reaction; good conditioner for stance stamina.

This is a quick conditioning drill that we work into practice occasionally to help strengthen the legs to play defense. The players line up along the baseline ready to participate in a four-quarter "game of agility." On the whistle, the players rapid fire, keeping their head up, knees bent, and base wide, with the weight on the balls of the feet. When the coach points, the players react by jump turning in that direction and then immediately back squared to the coach. During this jump turn, the players must maintain proper balance by staying in their stance and keeping the base wide. The players keep reacting to this directional pointing until the coach raises both hands over his head to signal the players to sprint to the other end of the court and back. Upon returning to the baseline, the second quarter begins immediately with rapid fire.

Our players come to realize that solid team efforts in this drill produce short, well-played agility games, while half-hearted or tired efforts make for longer games, sometimes resulting in overtime play to extract positive results.

Emphasize: Team effort, feet off the floor in rapid fire, relax the upper body (no fists).

Figure-eight drill.   Teaches defensive slide, conditioning.

See Diagram 3-13. Players line up at the corner of the baseline and sprint to half-court, slide across the midcourt line, sprint to the baseline, slide back across the endline, backpedal to midcourt, slide across the midcourt line, backpedal to the baseline, and finally, slide across the baseline to finish at the point where they started. We have found that two or three times through, done correctly, is a sufficient daily dose of this drill.

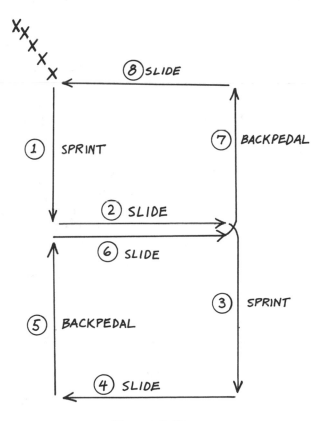

Diagram 3-13

All players are involved at once, with each waiting for the player in front of him to reach the 28-foot hash mark before starting his initial sprint. With players spread out in this drill, there will be instances where players are sprinting and back-pedaling toward one another. The player sprinting must communicate to the backpedaler and adjust his position to avoid any contact. At each turn we have our players hit the floor on the corners determined by the lines on the floor and yell "Defense!" This helps to generate a defensive pride throughout the team and also eliminates cutting corners from players trying to shorten the drill. "There are no short cuts to success."

Emphasize: Keep feet apart—we are looking for foot quickness, not speed at getting across the floor. Keep the upper body loose, work just as hard during the last slide as the first.

Transition drill. This drill deals with changing directions in defensive sliding, conditioning.

Players line up in a defensive stance with their feet perpendicular to the baseline and all facing in the same direction. On the whistle, they all start sliding down the court making sure that they keep their heads up, arms out with palms up, and feet apart at all times. On the next whistle they change direction and head back to where they just came. This transition is most effectively accomplished with a push off the outside foot and the initial step made with the foot closer to the direction called for. The whistle keeps blowing and players continue to change direction until the coach yells, "Baseline and back" and blows the whistle one final time to start them sprinting down the court to the opposite endline and back to the baseline they started from. This is a good drill to throw into practice now and then to keep the players' minds on defense.

Emphasize: Keep feet apart, stay low. We are not concerned with speed; foot quickness is the objective.

A Word About Off-the-Ball Defense

As has been mentioned before, stopping ball penetration is a team effort. All defensive players off-the-ball are constantly aware of their man's relationship to the ball and maintain a position to best deny ball penetration to the basket.

FUNDAMENTAL 2: CONTESTING THE STRONG-SIDE PASS

One concern that persists in the team man-to-man defense is to deny passes that create an advantage for the offense. One such pass is the strong-side guard-to-forward pass that moves the basketball closer to the basket.

Proper Technique

To combat this situation, the defender of the strong-side forward must overplay his man in what we call the ball-you-man position. (See Photo 9.) This calls for the defender to be one step off his man

Photo 9
Strong-side denial.

toward the ball with his inside foot up. His inside arm is extended with the hand in the passing lane and the palm open with the thumb pointing down. We react to offensive movement with quick defensive slides by the feet to maintain this ball-you-man position. This, along with tough on-the-ball defense, should make the guard-to-forward penetrating pass a difficult one to complete.

A move that the offensive player will use to offset this pressure is the backdoor cut. We continue to deny our opponent until he nears the foul lane to where we consider him in the low post area. At this time we open to the ball by pivoting on the foot closer to the basket and defend this man as if we were fronting the low post. The defender's head is now on a swivel, finding both the ball and his man. If he sees his man going through the lane to the weak side, he simply steps to the middle of the court to assume weak-side help position. If he should flash back out to the strong side, denial position is reestablished.

Drills for Denying the Strong-Side Pass

Denial slide drill. This drill teaches denial stance and movement.

See Diagram 3-14. The coach stands at the top of the key with the players lining up on one of the wings. The first player gets into a denial stance and starts sliding toward the lane. The coach points in alternating directions with the player reacting to the coach's signals. After a series of shuffles, the coach gives "the thumb" telling this player to slide to the lane, open up, and go through. When he gets to the other side, he immediately reas-

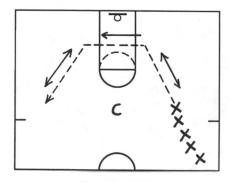

Diagram 3-14

sumes the denial position and reacts to the coach's directional pointing. This continues until he gets "the thumb" from the coach to exit the drill.

It is important to stress proper denial stance in this drill. Each player must have his hips closed with the inside foot up and back toward the ball. The inside hand is extended outward and the knees stay bent throughout. The feet are wider than the shoulders, lowering the center of gravity, and making it possible to change directions immediately when the coach points the other way.

Emphasize: Proper stance, wide base: quick feet, stay down, keep the knees bent.

Deny drill.   This drill teaches strong-side pass denial.

See Diagram 3-15. The players line up on the baseline with the first player stepping out as defender and the next player assuming the position of strong-side forward. The coach has the ball on the same side of the court above the foul line extended. The offensive player moves back and forth in an attempt to get a pass from the coach, while the defender stays in a position to deny the pass. Passes thrown by the coach are immediately returned to him and the drill continues.

The defender must maintain a proper defensive stance throughout the drill. It is important for him to stay lower than the offensive player to gain a slight edge in quickness needed to offset his opponent's advantage of knowing where he is going. It

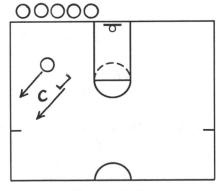

Diagram 3-15

is also necessary for the defender in denial to keep the offensive player away from his body. He tries to stay one step off his man toward the ball. One arm is extended into the passing lane, and the other is used to feel for his man and also to keep him away. When the offensive player moves toward the defender's body, the defender must slide with his feet in an attempt to maintain advantageous position. He must also use his arm nearest his opponent by flexing it horizontally out away from the body to ward him off.

Defending the Backdoor Cut

After a period of time, the coach signals with his head for the offensive player to go backdoor. The defender maintains his denial stance until he nears the lane, pivots on his inside foot, and extends both arms to get wide and cut down the passing lanes. His head moves to find his man, then the ball, then his man, as his feet move to secure position: (1) guarding the low post if that is where his man stays, (2) on the midline of the court if his man goes through to the weak side, or (3) back to denial if the offensive man pops back out on the strong side. On the pass after the offensive player has entered the middle of the court, the players go one-on-one to conclude the drill. The players then rotate from offense to defense to the end of the line.

Emphasize: Stay low, see the ball, open up to the ball when you reach the low post area.

FUNDAMENTAL 3: HELP AND RECOVERY

Another important part of the team man-to-man defense is *help and recovery*. This refers to off-the-ball defenders moving to help stop dribble penetration to the basket, then recovering to cover their own men. This occurs on the strong side in an effort to force the ball wide and to deny middle penetration. It happens on the weak side every time we rotate to stop strong-side penetration.

Our players realize that stopping the ball is our top priority, so they must always be in position to help stop penetration to the basket. Penetration that does occur must be met by off-the-ball defenders who are close enough to the line of attack to step in before the man reaches the basket. All players must understand the importance of help and recovery and be proficient at it to provide the support system that is needed for this defense to work.

We have established the following help and recovery rules that assist our players in mastering the skills and know-how of this phase of our defense:

1. Step to the ball. Any time a player is guarding the man with the ball and he passes, the defender must immediately step to the ball. While the ball is in the air the defender takes one step toward the direction of the pass to put himself in a position between the ball and his man and ready to help on any dribble penetration his way.

2. Always see the ball and man. Players can't react to ball penetration if they don't see it. All players on the court must see the ball and align themselves according to its location. In the event that the ball is closer to the basket than the man being guarded, the defender must sag to a position that will allow him to step in and stop dribble penetration.

3. Players who move to help must stop the ball. Once a player leaves his man to deny dribble penetration, he takes on the responsibility of stopping the ball. To accomplish this he must fully step in and take the charge if necessary. When the ball is picked up, a deny call follows with the defender staying with this man until he gives up the ball.

4. Once the ball is stopped and given up, the defender must recover to his man. If the man is the recipient of the release pass, the recovery has to be made while the ball is in the air. Any time this man rolls to the basket, we rely on our weakside help to pick him up.

Positional Responsibilities for Help and Recovery

Guard to guard: See Diagram 3-16. The defender on the guard without the ball is in position and ready to help if the

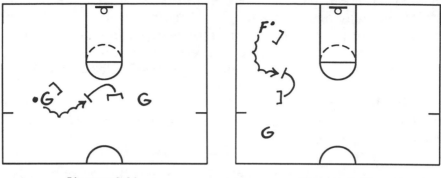

Diagram 3-16   **Diagram 3-17**

strong-side guard is beaten to the middle. We usually end up switching in this situation.

Guard to forward: See Diagram 3-17. When the ball is in the forward's hands, the strong-side guard sags to a point where he can help on penetration over the top to the middle.

Forward to guard: See Diagram 3-18. Normally this would be a deny situation for the defensive forward unless the ball is closer to the basket than his man. The on-the-ball defender forcing the ball wide knows he will receive help—the defensive forward must be there to deliver.

Guard or forward to center: See Diagram 3-19. Any time the ball is passed into the post area, all perimeter defenders

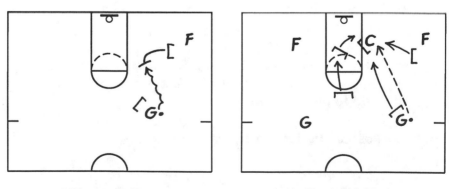

Diagram 3-18   **Diagram 3-19**

collapse on the ball. The ball is now in a high-percentage scoring area and needs our full attention. In this situation we would like nothing better than for the post player to kick the ball back outside where we can attempt to recover on the pass.

Drills for Help and Recovery

Note: With a little imagination, help and recovery respon-sibilities can be worked into many defensive drills. For example, in the deny drill, if the coach dribbles to the basket, the defending forward must step in to stop the ball, then recover to his man when the coach passes the ball to him.

Two-on-one drill. Teaches the specific slides involved in help and recovery.

See Diagram 3-20. A good way to teach help and recovery to players is to set up a two-on-one situation where the defender must move first to stop the ball and then to recover his man. In this drill, the two offensive players line up on the perimeter with the ball in the hands of the player farthest from the basket and the defender on the player without the ball. The action starts with the uncovered player dribbling toward the basket. The defender must step into the path of the dribbler to make him pick up his dribble and dish to his teammate. On the pass, the defender recovers to his man and forces him wide as they play one-on-one to conclude the drill.

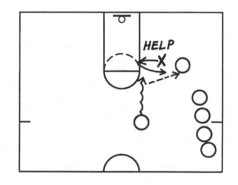

Diagram 3-20

We tell the player who starts the drill with the ball to dribble directly toward the basket. If the defender doesn't step in the way, dribble in for a lay-up. When the defender gets in proper position, we want this player to pass the ball out to the other player rather than attempt to dribble around him. Once this player passes the ball, he is no longer involved in the drill. The rotation in this drill goes from offensive wing to defensive wing to the end of the line with the other offensive position being manned by the coach or players who have already completed the drill.

Emphasize: Stop the ball—draw a charge if necessary, move to your man while the ball is in the air.

Two-on-two help and recovery.   Teaches help and recovery while simulating game conditions.

See Diagram 3-21. Players line up on the sideline with the first two players stepping out as defenders and the next two as offensive players. The two offensive players take their positions on the same side of the court, with the ball in the hands of the guard. The two defenders align themselves accordingly with X1 forcing the guard to dribble wide and X2 in a deny stance against the forward. We want the guard in this drill to dribble toward the baseline to make X2 stop him. His rule is to dribble until X2 makes

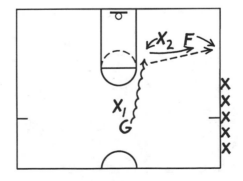

Diagram 3-21

him stop. If X2 doesn't step in adequately, this man must dribble in for the lay-up. While the guard dribbles, we want his teammate to pop out to the corner. After the guard picks up his dribble, he tosses it to the forward, forcing X2 to quickly recover. The forward, upon receiving the pass, drives to the basket with X2 forcing baseline and X1 providing support. Any time the ball is stopped and passed to the other player, the nearest defender calls "I've got ball!" and attacks the ballhandler, while the other defender moves to an area of support.

Emphasize: The man with the ball is the number one priority.

Step-to-the-ball drill. Teaches players to immediately assume help and recovery responsibilities once their man gives up the ball.

See Diagram 3-22. The players line up out front, with the first player stepping out on defense and the second player on offense. The drill starts with the offensive player passing the ball to the coach, who is located at the wing position. While the pass is in the air, the defender takes one quick step to the ball. The offensive player tries to cut in front of the defensive player en route to the basket, but the defender works to force his man to go behind him so that he can maintain the ball-you-man position that is so important in our defense. The offensive player heads to the low block and attempts to post up with the defender moving in front of him to deny him a pass in this area. Once the defense

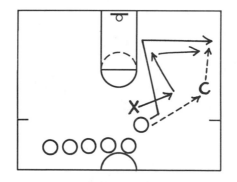

Diagram 3-22

has good position, the offensive player will pop out to the strong-side corner, forcing the defensive player into a deny position. Any pass to the offense in this drill results in a one-on-one situation that is played until the defense gets the ball, the ball goes out of bounds, or the offense scores. Rotation is again from offense to defense to the end of the line.

Emphasize: Step to the ball while the ball is in the air, always stay between your man and the ball, see the ball, feel for your man.

Collapse drill. This drill works with the perimeter collapse to the middle.

See Diagram 3-23. Any time the ball is passed into the post area, the players on the perimeter must drop to the ball to help out. We work with our players to make this drop a calculated and effective one, not a reckless charge to the ball.

This drill starts with offensive players at the wing and low post, with the wing defender in proper defensive position and the post defender behind his man. Normally we front the post when the ball is in this location, but we realize that there will be times when the offensive player posts us up.

The wing starts with the ball and throughout this drill is limited to one dribble per possession. We want this player to initiate the action by passing the ball into the low post. The wing defender's first job is to harass this entry pass, getting a piece of it if possible. While the ball is in flight to the low post, the defender

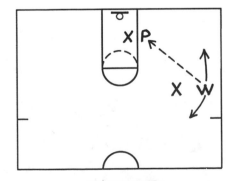

Diagram 3-23

turns and sprints to double team the ball. This turn is made in the direction that the ball goes by the defender (i.e., over the left shoulder, turn to the left), and the sprint inside is made with the hands up in an attempt to encourage the post player to pass the ball back outside. We would rather take our chances with the outside shot than with an attempt from the high-percentage scoring area in the lane. The wing defender must react to the pass outside by turning in the direction of the pass and moving toward his man's outside shoulder to force him baseline. The wing may shoot, use his one dribble to set up a shot, or dump the ball back into the low post. These players continue to play two-on-two until the defense comes up with the ball, the ball goes out of bounds, or the offense scores. Rotation is from offense to defense to the end of the line.

Emphasize: Protect the middle, force the pass back outside.

FUNDAMENTAL 4: TAKING THE CHARGE

Any defense that relies on support from off the ball defenders must have players willing to step in to take the charge. We talk about this fundamental often at practice so that our players realize its importance within the framework of the defense. Enthusiastic team responses now greet each offensive foul that is absorbed by any of our players. Willingness to take a charge is an integral part of our defense because it is the "help" that we promise our players when they force their men wide with the ball. Players who step up to help and then step away to avoid contact cause a breakdown in the system. Those who stand there and force the offensive player to pick up his dribble, even if it means taking a charge, are the players we want on the court. (See Photo 10.)

Taking the charge is the most effective play in basketball. The player who steps in to take a charge:

1. Causes the offense to turn the ball over without a field goal attempt.
2. Frustrates not only the player whistled for the foul, but the entire offense.

Photo 10
Players off the ball must be willing to step in to take the charge.

3. Makes the offense hesitant about driving to the hoop again (more so than the blocked shot) because of the fear of picking up another foul.
4. Exhibits a commitment to defense and a toughness in character that may work to intimidate the offense.

Proper Technique

Time must be spent teaching players how to take a charge. Players aware of the proper techniques of taking the charge will be less hesitant and more willing to step in when the situation calls for it.

First and foremost, each player must understand that to draw a charge, he must first beat the offensive player to a spot and then hold his position. If contact results, we want the offensive player to be moving and the defensive player stationary, clearly depicting to the official an offensive charge. If the offensive player changes his course of action, the defender remains stationary, satisfied to force an off-balanced shot or a change of direction with the dribble. A cardinal sin for the defender in this situation is to move into contact—this will invariably result in a defensive blocking foul.

Next, players must know how to absorb contact appropriately to avoid injury. In bracing for contact we tell our players to keep a wide base with the knees bent. Contact is to be absorbed by the chest first, and on feeling contact, the player "gives" and falls straight back landing on the seat of his pants. The hands are not utilized to brace the fall, but come into use to help the player get back up. We caution our players not to fall back before contact is made as this will cause the initial impact to be somewhere other than the chest area. Much time is spent describing to our players when and how to take the charge. To provide practical applications of this situation, we use occasional "charge" drills in practice.

Drills for Drawing the Charge

Any time we set up a charge drill, we want to make it a practical part of the team man-to-man defense. Another consideration is that we don't want the offensive player to build up a full head of steam before contact, so we try to limit him to one or two dribbles before he reaches the spot designated for contact.

Step-in drill. Teaches beating the player to a spot to draw the charge.

See Diagram 3-24. The coach stands in front with the ball and two players step out to the wing—one on offense and the other his defender. The coach initiates the drill by dribbling toward the hoop, forcing the defender to step in to deny penetration. Meanwhile, his man drifts to the corner to be in position for a pass from the coach once his dribble has been stopped. Upon receiving the pass from the coach, this player dribbles straight to the basket, going right through the defender if he were in the way. The defender, after stopping the coach's dribble, recovers to his man once the pass is thrown. Seeing his man dribble toward the basket, he now must beat him to a spot along the way and draw the charge. After contact, we evaluate the situation and then rotate the players from offense to defense to the end of the line.

Emphasize: Hold your ground, don't lean to either side to force contact, "give" immediately on contact.

Charge drill. Teaches players proper techniques in taking the charge.

See Diagram 3-25. Players line up on the baseline with an offensive player in the corner and a defender on the midline of the

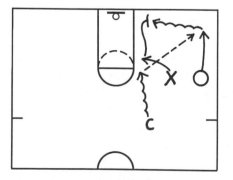

Diagram 3-24

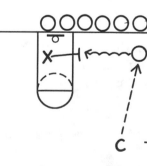

Diagram 3-25

court as if guarding a weak-side forward. The coach passes the ball to the forward to start the drill. Upon receiving the pass, the player dribbles to the hoop. The defender reacts by moving over to beat him to the low block. The offensive player does not try to avoid the defense, instead he goes right through him in an attempt to score. The defender must hold his ground and draw the charge. Each successful drawn charge is met by an enthusiastic response from the players along the baseline, while illegal blocks are discussed and corrected. Players once again rotate from offense to defense to the end of the line.

Emphasize: Lean your chest in so it is the first part of the body to be hit, don't fall back before contact.

FUNDAMENTAL 5: PLAYING THE WEAK SIDE

We tell the defenders on the ball that they have the most important job in this defense, but their efforts would be futile without an effective support system behind them. The weak-side players are the backbone of the team man-to-man defense. We want the on-the-ball defenders to apply constant pressure and force penetration along the baseline. We rely on the weak-side players to have the toughness and tenacity to step in and shut off all routes of penetration to the basket.

Any time the ball is not in the middle of the court, our players become strong-side, post, or weak-side defenders. Responsibilities vary depending upon the location of the ball and the man being guarded. Players on the opposite side of the court, or the weak side, do not pose immediate penetration problems, so our weak-side defenders sag to the middle. Guarding a man who is away from the ball does not provide this defender a rest—rather, it allows him the opportunity to move to the middle to be in a position to help, or support, the defender on the ball and any teammate defending the post.

Proper Technique

To be effective in this position, players must maintain a stance of quickness, with the knees bent and weight on the balls of their feet. The weak-side defender must open to the ball, with the strong-side hand pointing to the ball and the weak-side hand pointing to his man. These hands are like antennae, moving whenever the ball or man moves to keep the brain informed of any adjustments that have to be made with the feet. These hands are also ready to steal or deflect any pass through the middle to his man. Passes that go through the middle of this defense are deadly and cannot be allowed. Only passes that are lobbed can go cross-court, as these allow the weak-side and all other defenders to react while the ball is in the air to assume new strong-side and weak-side positions.

Drills to Teach Weak-Side Defense

Weak-side recognition drill. Teaches proper defensive positioning and weak-side rotation techniques.

See Diagram 3-26. This is a drill that we use to teach proper alignment in our defense. Five offensive players line up around the perimeter with a player in each corner, one on each wing, and a point guard. Two defenders step out to guard the wing and forward on the same side. All offensive players remain in their general areas with the defensive players reacting on every pass to maintain proper defensive positioning. The ball starts at the point with the defender on the wing concerned about his man—in a denial position as long as his man is closer to the basket than the ball. The defender on the forward moves about two steps to the ball in anticipation of helping to stop any penetration into the middle.

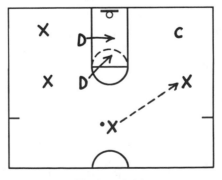

Diagram 3-26

The ball is passed around the perimeter and the defenders react by moving to their proper position on the court. If the first pass should go to the guarded wing, the on-the-ball defender assumes a defensive stance that will force the ball wide, while the corner defender moves to a denial stance. A pass to the strong-side corner would result in the defensive forward forcing baseline and the defensive guard in a help and recovery position. Any pass to the opposite side of the court calls for both defenders to move quickly to weak-side defensive position with one foot over the midline of the court. Defensive position is realigned every time the ball moves. We usually station the coach in the opposite corner and end each time through the drill with the coach dribbling baseline, forcing the weak-side defenders to rotate to stop the dribble (Diagram 3-27).

It is essential that both weak-side defenders react immediately to the dribble so that the weak-side forward can beat the dribbler to a spot outside the lane and the weak-side guard is in position to shut off the cross-court pass.

Emphasize: Whenever the ball moves—you move! Move while the ball is in flight, see the ball at all times.

Weak-side transition drill.   Reviews on-the-ball rules with a transition to weak-side defense.

See Diagram 3-28. The players line up on the sideline with the first two players stepping out on defense and the next two on offense. The offensive players take positions on the same side of

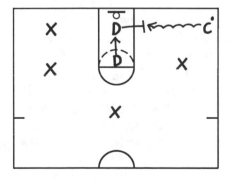

Diagram 3-27

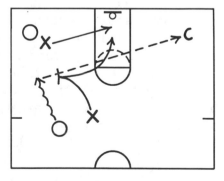

Diagram 3-28

the court with the ball in the guard's hands. The coach takes a position in the opposite corner.

The drill starts with the players playing two-on-two basketball. The defensive guard forces the dribbler wide and the defensive forward gets into a position to help if needed. We have a rule in this drill that the offensive player without the ball must stay out of the middle. The only way middle penetration can occur is through the dribble and, once in the middle, the offense can shoot. On the coach's command of "Ball!" the ball is passed cross-court to him. The defenders react by moving to weak-side defensive positions while the ball is in the air. The offensive players (now both without the ball and forbidden from the middle), remain active, moving back and forth, switching positions, to force their defenders to constantly adjust their positions. The coach may try to pass the ball through the defenders if an opening to an offensive player shows. The defenders, however, should be in a position to deflect or steal this pass and return it to the coach. The coach ends the drill by dribbling baseline, forcing a rotation, then passing to one of the offensive players. This results in either a steal by the defense or a two-on-two situation played to a conclusion.

Emphasize: Maintain a position where you can see both your man and the ball, point with both hands.

Weak-side close-out drill.   Teaches shutting off the baseline drive and reacting to a pass thrown to the open man.

See Diagram 3-29. This drill is run with two offensive players and two defenders. One offensive player has the ball, and he lines up on the side of the court about halfway up the lane. His teammate stands just outside the opposite elbow. One defender plays on the ball and is responsible for forcing the dribbler baseline. The other defender assumes a weak-side defensive position as if he were guarding a player in the opposite corner (who doesn't exist in this drill). The drill starts with the ballhandler dribbling to the basket. The weak-side defender moves on the dribble to shut off the baseline penetration before the ball reaches the lane, and both defenders then combine to put the dribbler in jail. Through our rotation system, we know that the weak-side guard will move down to close off the passing lane

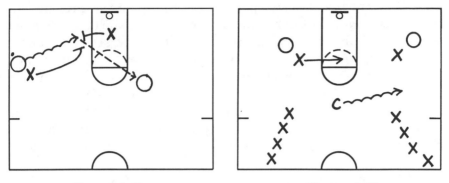

Diagram 3-29   Diagram 3-30

cross-court to the weak-side forward's man. This leaves the pass to the weak-side guard's man as a viable option if it is recognized by the offense. We must practice this possibility.

The defenders must first combine to shut off penetration to the basket, then do their best to limit the passing lane to the open player at the elbow. With the dribble used up, both defenders can bring up their arms in an effort to deflect or steal any pass, but both must maintain a wide base and bent knees to not allow the player in jail to pivot out of trouble. Once the pass is made to the elbow, the nearest defender sprints out, calls out "I've got ball!" and the players proceed to play two-on-two basketball until the defense comes up with the ball or the offense scores.

Emphasize: Always force the ball wide, react immediately to any pass.

Strong-side/weak-side drill. This drill teaches denial and weak-side defense.

See Diagram 3-30. The players form lines on each side of the court, the first player in each line stepping out on defense and the next on offense. The offensive players set up on opposite wings and the defenders take up a deny position with the ball in the coach's hands out beyond the top of the key. The coach moves to one side, and the defender on that side continues to deny his man while the other defender moves to the middle where he straddles the lane in weak-side help position.

We want the offensive players to remain on their respective sides of the court but to remain active, making the defense move to maintain proper position. Any time the coach sees the opportunity, he throws a chest or bounce pass to an open player. By our defensive rules, neither of these passes should get through. We want the defender to deflect or steal the ball and return it to the coach. If the pass gets through, the offense takes it to the basket in an attempt to score. When the play ends, the ball is thrown back out to the coach and the drill continues with the same four players.

Throughout the drill, the coach moves from side to side providing the opportunity for both defenders to practice denial and weak-side help. We especially like this drill because with a few adjustments, most facets of our defense can be worked on. For example, the coach dribbles toward the hoop and both defenders must help and recover. Or the coach goes low on one side and the offensive player picks away, forcing the defense to switch and pick up the flashing post.

The drill concludes when the coach shoots, forcing the defenders to work on yet another fundamental—boxing out. If the offense gets the rebound, they take it right back strong to the basket. When the defense gets the coach's rebound, the drill ends and we rotate offense to defense to the end of the line.

Emphasize: See the ball at all times, every time your man moves—you move, keep the knees bent and hands ready at all times.

Two-on-two weak-side drill. This drill teaches weak-side help.

See Diagram 3-31. Another drill that we use to practice weak-side defense is a two-on-two drill with special restrictions put on the offense to ensure that weak-side help comes into play. The players line up at half-court, with the first two players once again on defense and the next two on offense. They will play two-on-two starting at the hash mark (28-foot line) with the following rules for the offense:

1. Both players stay on their own sides of the court. They may drive to the middle with the ball, but they are not allowed in this area without the ball.

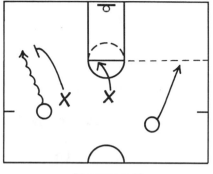

Diagram 3-31

2. All (cross-court) passes must be made laterally or away from the basket.

3. The offensive player without the ball is not allowed below the free-throw line extended.

By establishing these rules, we know that there will at all times be a defender in weak-side help position. This player will move as the ball moves to maintain a proper relationship to both. If the ball is dribbled over-the-top to the middle, he steps in to help and recover. If his teammate is successful in forcing penetration along the baseline, he rotates to stop the dribbler outside of the lane, then reacts to a pass to the opposite elbow area. This drill continues until the offense scores or the defense comes up with the ball.

Emphasize: Always see both your man and the ball—point to both, react to any pass while it is in the air.

FUNDAMENTAL 6: DEFENDING THE FLASH CUT

All offenses use the flash cut in one way or another in an attempt to get the ball inside to the high-percentage area. The flash cut, by our definition, occurs any time a weak-side player moves from the weak side to the three-second area, thus changing his status to an inside post player who needs our full attention. It is extremely important that he is met and denied access to the ball by his defender.

Proper Technique

The weak-side defender must be constantly aware of where both his man and the ball are. Any time his man moves to the middle of the court, this defender must step up with his inside foot to establish a position of denial—the base kept wide, knees bent, and inside hand in the passing lane. The other arm is used as a bar to keep the cutter away from his body, and the feet move to beat this player to a spot, forcing him to alter his destination. Effectively shutting off the flash cut will force the offensive player to back cut to the basket. This move is countered by the defender opening to the ball and fronting the offensive man down the lane, using his hands and a swiveling head to stay aware of his man's location. If the offensive man then retreats to the weak side, the defender reestablishes weak-side help position. If the offensive player chooses to move to the strong-side corner, the defender steps up in a denial position to prevent pass penetration.

Drills to Teach Defending the Flash Cut

Cut-off drill. This drill is set up to improve position and techniques necessary for stopping the flash cut.

See Diagram 3-32. The players line up on the baseline. The first player steps out as the defender and the next player in line as an offensive forward. The coach has the ball and is located on the opposite side of the court halfway down the lane, requiring the defender to assume weak-side position.

The offensive player starts by moving up and down the weak side, forcing his defender to move to maintain proper position. The coach will throw a chest or bounce pass through the middle any time he feels the defender is improperly aligned. The offensive player next flashes to the ball, and the defender steps up to beat this player to a spot, forcing him to alter his course across the lane. The offensive player adjusts his cut, and the defender reacts to keep an advantageous position between the man and the ball. Any time the offensive player opens up, the coach feeds him

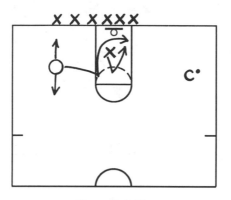

Diagram 3-32

for a shot at the basket. We limit the offensive player's effort to three seconds in the lane, and if the defender is effective in shutting off the passing lane to him, he retreats back to the weak side and flashes again. This continues with the defender staying low and wide to thwart all attempts of the offensive player to get open in the middle.

The drill ends with the coach dribbling baseline and the defender moving over to stop dribble penetration. The coach then flips the ball to the offensive player (who has drifted away from the basket) and the defender reacts by closing out the ball. The players then play one-on-one to a conclusion.

Emphasize: Use your arms to keep the player off your body and your hands to "keep in touch" with him while he is in the middle.

Z drill. This drill teaches stepping to the ball, weak-side positioning, and defending the flash cut.

See Diagram 3-33. This drill starts just above the top of the key, with a player holding the basketball in triple threat position and a defender squared up in a stance to force the ball out of the middle. The coach lines up at a wing ready to accept a pass from the point. We will allow the offensive player up to three dribbles to beat the defender across the foul line. If this occurs, the dribbler

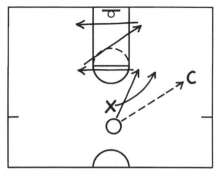

Diagram 3-33

continues to the hoop for the easy score and the drill restarts with the same two players. If the ballhandler is unable to cross the foul line after three dribbles or simply chooses to pass to the coach without using his allotment of dribbles, the defender reacts by stepping to the ball to immediately get into a ball-you-man position to prevent any give and go to the basket.

On the pass, the offensive player will move to the strong-side elbow looking for a return pass from the coach. If he doesn't show, he runs a Z: a movement along the foul line to the weak-side elbow, then a diagonal cut to the low block, followed by movement away from the ball to the weak corner. Any time during this Z-cut the coach will throw a chest or bounce pass inside if the offensive player opens up. If the Z cut is completed without a pass, the offensive player will then flash cut to the ball, looking for a pass from the coach. We waive the three-second rule in this drill, forcing the defender to work extra hard to keep his man from showing inside. Once the ball is passed inside, the players go one-on-one to conclude the drill.

In this drill we are concerned with defensive movement and keeping proper relationship to the man and the ball at all times. Any time the offensive player moves to the ball (as in the initial cut or the flash cut in this drill), the defender must step in to deny, hold his ground, and force his man to change direction.

Any time the offensive player slides down the lane to the low post (as in the diagonal cut in this drill), the defender must adjust with his feet to front the player as he approaches the midline of the court and continue to front as this player moves toward the low block. At all times the defender is aware of ball location. If the ball remains above the foul line he denies the low post; if it is below the foul line he maintains his fronting position.

Any time the offensive player heads away from the ball, the defender follows him only to the midline of the court, stopping there to assume weak-side help position ready to adjust to any movement of the ball or his man.

Emphasize: Step to the ball, not the basket, see the ball, don't let up—stay in your stance throughout the drill, step in and use the arm bar to defend the flash cutter.

FUNDAMENTAL 7: DEFENDING THE LOW POST

Offensive players who set up on the low block pose a constant problem to any defense. Penetrating passes to this position force the defense to collapse and allow the offense a high-percentage scoring opportunity so close to the basket. One of the major building blocks of the team man-to-man defense is a commitment to keep the ball out of the low post area. Our rules of forcing the ball wide and sagging on the weak side are geared to meet this objective. To complete the package, all players must be taught how to individually defend an opponent stationed on the low block.

Proper Technique

Our low post coverage rules are determined by the location of the ball. As long as the ball is in the middle or on the opposite side of the court, this defender sags off his man toward the ball to be in a position to both help his teammates and defend the flash cut. We will not overconcern ourselves with this player as long ás he is more than one pass away.

We get serious in a hurry when the ball enters the same side of the court as the low block player. His defender must immediately assume a deny position one step toward the ball with the inside foot up and inside arm out just as if he were guarding a forward on the strong side. We will stay with this denial coverage of the post as long as the ball remains above the foul line extended.

When the ball is dribbled or passed below the foul line extended, the passing angle to the low post greatly increases, along with our defensive intensity. We now have this defender front the post and use weak-side players to support any pass over the top. (See Photo 11.) This move from deny to front must be done with quick feet in order to avoid getting pinned by the post player. We tell this defender to initiate this move by stepping through with his foot nearer the post player. This foot must be placed in front of his opponent's inside foot allowing him to shuffle in front with both hands held high and contact made with the butt to monitor location. In the event that contact is lost, the defender quickly turns his head and feels with his arms to relocate his man.

Occasionally our players are pinned by an alert post player who steps up with the inside foot and uses his inside arm to ward off the defender. When this occurs, the defender must quickly slide behind the post player to the baseline side, set up in a deny stance with the back to the baseline, and then step up to front when the opportunity allows. Defenders who get pinned must adjust by starting higher on the post player the next time down the floor.

Drills to Teach Defending the Low Post

Defend-the-post drill.   Teaches defensive footwork on the low post player.

See Diagram 3-34. Players line up on the baseline. One player steps out as post player and another as post defender. Two other players are selected to stand out on the perimeter in the guard and forward positions on the same side of the court. This drill was designed with our forwards and centers in mind, but often we will include the guards because we feel it is important for all players on the team to learn to defend this area of the court.

The drill starts with the ball in the guard's hands above the foul line extended and the post defender in a deny stance with his inside foot up and inside hand out to deny the passing lane to his

Photo 11
Defending the low post when the ball is below the foul line.

man. On the pass to the forward, the defender steps through with his back foot and "steps over" his man to a fronting position. A pass back to the guard calls for a reversal of this procedure to reassume the denial stance.

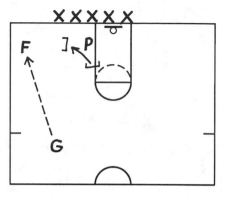

Diagram 3-34

At the beginning of the drill, the post player remains stationary to allow the defender to work on the footwork necessary to shut down passing lanes to this area. Once we feel the defender has mastered the footwork, we play for real. The guard and forward pass back and forth, trying to create an open pass into the post. Any chest or bounce pass to the post player results in one-on-one action to the basket. The defender's goal is to keep the ball out of the post player's hands for 30 seconds.

We will occasionally adjust this drill by adding a weak-side defender and then allowing the perimeter players to lob the ball into the post area. Another adjustment that can be made is to move the post player up to the medium post and working the defender to gain proficiency in defending this position as well.

Emphasize: Move while the ball is in the air, footwork must be quick, maintain contact with the post at all times.

Post-to-post drill. Teaches low post and flash cut defense.

See Diagram 3-35. In this drill we start by taking four players and positioning them around the perimeter without any defense. Two other players then step out to the low post area with one setting up as the fifth offensive player and the other as his defender. We tell the defender to deny all passes to the post.

The ball starts in the guard's hands with the post defender in a deny position. This defender must step to the ball on all

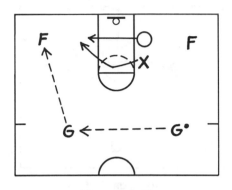

Diagram 3-35

passes. If the ball goes to the strong-side corner, stepping to the ball leads to fronting the post player. This is the position we want our post defenders in when the ball is in the corner. Any pass back to the guard or over to the weak side is also countered by the post defender stepping to the ball. This will allow this defender to stay between his man and the ball at all times to shut off the passing lane and also to prevent his man from flash cutting to the ball.

The ball is passed around the perimeter until the post player opens up for a chest or bounce pass. Once this occurs and the ball is thrown inside, the defender plays one-on-one defense against the post player.

Emphasize: Move the feet while the ball is in the air, keep the body between the ball and the opponent at all times.

Two-on-two post drill. Teaches low post defense, flash cut defense, and works with switching underneath off the ball.

See Diagram 3-36. Two players step to the low blocks as offensive postmen with two defenders matching up to deny the ball to them inside. The coach has the ball in one of the corners, forcing one defender to front his man and the other to sag to provide weak-side help. The post player to the side of the ball tries to get the ball near the low block, while the weak-side player drifts up and down to keep his defender moving. The coach may try a chest, bounce, overhead, or lob pass to get the ball inside. Once the ball comes into the possession of the offensive player, he and his teammate go two-on-two to the basket.

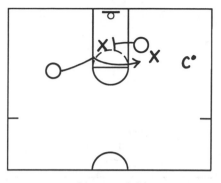

Diagram 3-36

If the low post defender shuts off the passing lane to the post, his man releases to the weak side and the two offensive players exchange positions. If a screen is involved during this transition, the two defenders switch to best prevent a pass to the strong-side post area. If there is no screen, each defender stays with his own man and employs the post rules that have been established.

If, after 30 seconds, the coach is unable to get the ball inside, he passes over the top of the defense to the weak-side player and the drill concludes with the players engaging in two-on-two to the hoop.

Emphasize: Front the low post; maintain contact at all times—know when the low post releases, communicate the "pick" and "switch."

FUNDAMENTAL 8: THE SWITCH

One of our basic rules in this defense is to switch on all screens on or off the ball. By utilizing this strategy, we avoid the confusion of whether or not to switch on certain screens. It is understood by all players that we will switch on all screens. At the core of this decision is the commitment to maintain maximum pressure on the ball and on players off the ball moving to advantageous positions. By switching, we force teams away from the purpose of the screen to second and third options that aren't as familiar. To ensure the effectiveness of this approach, we must work to teach the players how to properly perform this fundamental.

Proper Technique

Effective switching begins with communication. The defender whose man sets the screen must warn his targeted teammate as soon as possible. This is done with a simple "pick" call that indicates to the teammate that a screen is coming. Both players maintain proper defensive relationships on their men, but now anticipate a switch as a result of this screen.

As for on-the-ball screens, either defender may call "Switch," at which point the defender on the screener steps out to take on the dribbler and force him wide, adhering to our on-the-ball rules. The player getting screened must do his best to get behind the man rolling to the basket, then deny or front him depending upon the location of the ball. We rely on our on-the-ball pressure and weak-side help to support us during this vulnerable move. For screens away from the ball, the defender of the screeener switches to establish position dictated by our defensive rules and the player getting screened fights around his man to get in a proper ball-you-man position.

Drills to Teach the Switch

Pick and roll drill. Teaches the techniques involved in switching on screens.

See Diagram 3-37. Players line up in two lines on the sideline with the first two players stepping out as defenders and the next two as offensive guard and forward. The ball starts in the guard's hands, and the drill consists of live two-on-two action to the basket initiated by a screen from the forward. The defense must talk ("Pick–Switch" or "Pick–Stay") and react instantaneously to all decisions to force the ball wide and keep the screener from opening up in the middle on the roll.

Throughout this drill, it is important that players follow the defensive rules that have been set forth for the team man-to-man defense. Too often, the existence of a screen causes an overadjustment by the defense that leads to a breakdown in coverage. For

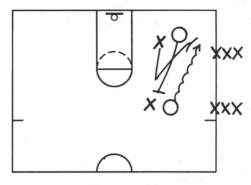

Diagram 3-37

example, the defender on the ball must force his man sideline and can't be intimidated by the screen to the point of allowing his man to penetrate over-the-top. We want our players to view the screen as a minor inconvenience that can be overcome with communication, quick feet, and little trouble.

The players go until the defense comes up with the ball or the offense scores, and we then rotate from offense to defense to the end of the line.

The following adjustments can enhance the production of this drill:

1. Run the drill from both sides of the court.
2. Start both lines out front and run the drill from the guard positions.
3. Start one offensive player at the low post area and the other in the corner. Have the post pick for the forward.

Emphasize: Talk—if either defender calls "Switch," this is the call we live with.

FUNDAMENTAL 9: BOXING OUT

No defensive effort is complete until provisions have been made to secure the rebound. All defensive players must react to any shot by anticipating a miss and working for position to grab the ball. We have found that players who rely strictly on their size or jumping ability in this endeavor fall way short of their potential to rebound. Those who constantly work for position on every shot are the players who are going to get the ball for us. We want all of our players, regardless of size, to realize the importance of rebounding position.

Proper Technique

Players must make contact with their opponents on every shot. Those closer to the basket will then pivot and box out while those away from the hoop follow the contact with a turn and sprint toward the middle to help in the rebounding action (check-and-go). We realize that most rebounds will fall near the basket, so most of our time is spent with players in the box-out area working on the rebounding pivot and box-out stance. (See Photo 12, page 98.)

Players in the box-out area react to all shots by first making contact with the hand or forearm and then pivoting to make a second and restraining contact with the butt. This pivot can be made in one of two ways:

1. *Inside pivot:* Defender faces his man to make contact on the shot. He then reacts to the direction his man takes to the basket by stepping through in front of his body with the opposite foot to turn and cut his opponent off (Diagram 3-38).

2. *Reverse pivot:* Defender faces his man and makes contact on the shot. He then reacts to the direction taken by his man by pivoting on the foot to that side, turning his back to his opponent, and finding him with the butt (Diagram 3-39).

While pivoting, we want the defender to keep the elbows as high as the shoulders and the hands with the fingers pointing upward ready to go for the ball. This makes the rebounder wider and more difficult to go around and keeps the hands up and off of any defenders. Once the pivot is complete, the feet must be as wide as the shoulders and the knees bent, making the legs ready to take the player to the ball. The head is up with the eyes focused on the rim. When the ball comes off the rim, the defender must go and get the ball, not wait for it to come to him. (See Photo 13, page 100.)

Photo 12
Players in the box-out area must establish and maintain contact: the feet are
shoulder-width apart and the hands are ready to go get the ball.

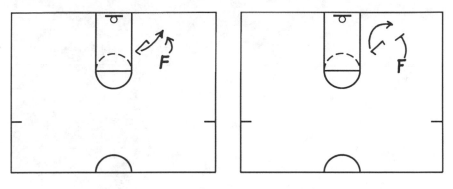

Diagram 3-38   Diagram 3-39

In the occasional event that the defender is caught fronting the low post on a shot, we have this player box his man in. This is done by placing one foot between the opponent's base and resting the thigh on the man's butt. The hands are raised high, in full view of the referee, and ready to tip or grab any ball that bounces in his direction. The defender must go straight up and use the leverage that has been established by the foot and thigh to prevent his opponent from jumping back to get the ball.

Drills for Boxing Out

Elbow rebounding drill. Teaches rebounding technique necessary for the box-out area. (See Diagram 3-40.)

Players form lines at each elbow, with the first player in each line stepping out as the defender/rebounder. The next player in line is the offensive player. He is allowed to "drift" down his side of the court while the coach holds on to the ball just beyond the foul line. When the coach finally shoots the ball, the defenders make contact with their men, then pivot to gain inside position. This is followed by an all-out effort to get the ball. If a defender gets the rebound, both defenders go to the end of the line and the offensive players now become defenders. If an offensive player gets the rebound, he and his teammate play two-on-two to the basket and, regardless of the outcome, there is no rotation. The same defenders go back to the elbows. Any shot made by the coach or ball knocked out-of-bounds by a defender also result in the

Photo 13
To ensure a possession, rebounders must go after the ball with both hands.

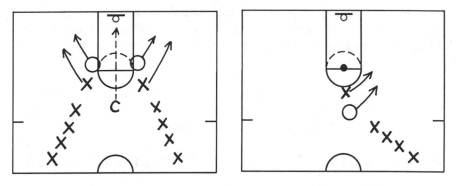

Diagram 3-40   Diagram 3-41

same defenders staying on to rebound. The only way defenders can move to the end of the line is by one of them rebounding the coach's shot.

Emphasize: Grab the rebound with two hands, keep the fingers up to make the hands ready.

Keep out drill. Teaches box-out area techniques.

See Diagram 3-41. The players line up out front with the first two players stepping to the top of the key to start the drill. The ball is placed on the foul line, and one player assumes the role of the defender and lines up with his heels on the circle at the top of the key facing away from the ball toward the other player. On the whistle, the offensive player tries to get the ball while his defender utilizes inside boxing out techniques to ward him off.

The coach counts out the seconds, and if the defender is successful in keeping his opponent away from the ball for a predetermined time he goes to the end of the line. We strive for three seconds early in the season and raise our goal to five seconds as the season wears on. If the offensive player does get to the ball, he picks it up and the two players go one-on-one to the basket. Regardless of the outcome, the same two players line up at the top of the key for a "rematch" with added pressure on the defender to keep his opponent from the ball. If the defender succeeds in his objective in the "rematch," he goes to the end of the line with no penalty. If the offensive player gets to the ball for a second time, the two again play one-on-one and the defender must then run laps—one for each possession and another for each score (maximum of four laps)—while the offensive player rotates to the defender's position.

Emphasize: Keep both elbows out to widen rebounding stance; maintain contact to feel offensive player's moves, then shuffle the feet to shut off his line to the ball.

Check-the-shooter drill.   Teaches check-and-go technique used on perimeter players.

See Diagram 3-42. Players line up on the baseline with the first two players stepping out to the corner or wing to initiate the drill. The coach has the ball out front and starts play by dribbling toward the basket, forcing the defender to help and recover. Upon seeing the defender move, the coach flips the ball to the offensive player who shoots right away before the defender can fully recover. As soon as the shooter's feet hit the floor, we want him to aggressively go after his shot. It is the defender's responsibility to not allow him to be a factor in the rebounding action.

Outside shooters, as well as other perimeter players, are defended by the check-and-go technique once a shot is released. We want to bring all five defenders to the basket to help rebound—maintaining contact to box out on the perimeter doesn't lead us to this objective. In this drill we want the defender to attack the ball, contest the shot as well as he can, and then work

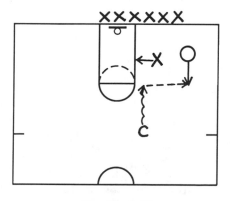

Diagram 3-42

to secure favorable position in the rebounding area. To do this he first makes contact with the player and reads which direction his first step to the basket is going in. The defender then pivots to get the inside track on his man and heads to the basket. Any contact that results from this pivot will help to slow down the offensive player's charge to the basket. We feel that perimeter contact is not as important as rebounding support, so we don't demand contact after the pivot in the check-and-go situation. Our goal is not to box out this player; rather it is to beat him to the middle where his defender can be in a position to help secure the rebound.

The drill ends when either the shot is made or the defender gets the rebound. An offensive rebound results in one-on-one action to the basket and then a repeat of the drill for the same two players.

Emphasize: Go after the ball, don't wait for it to come to you; hands ready—anticipate the quick rebound off the front rim.

Three-man survival drill.   Teaches the aggressiveness needed to be a good rebounder.

See Diagram 3-43. This is a good drill for instilling aggressiveness on the boards. Three players are selected and all take a place in the lane. The coach throws up a shot, and it is every man for himself on the rebound and put-back. The player who gets the ball must go against the other two players in an effort to score. There is no out-of-bounds in this drill, and action continues until

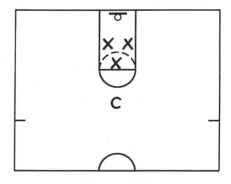

Diagram 3-43

one of the players score. This player is then replaced by the next player in line.

At one point we ran this drill with no rules and allowed all sorts of contact. Two problems evolved out of this approach that caused us to reconsider: (1) unlimited contact promoted bad defensive habits with defenders using their hands instead of their feet, and (2) the amount of contact created ill will between teammates. We have since "cleaned up" the drill by telling the defenders to follow the rules of our defense as well as they can and that minimal unintentional contact is all that will be allowed.

Emphasize: Go strong to the ball, grab the ball with two hands.

Weak-side box-out drill. Teaches the technique for rebounding from the weak-side position.

The weak-side box-out is perhaps one of the most important skills that must be taught to players in the team man-to-man defense. After the ball has been forced wide and the offensive team settles for a perimeter shot, chances are the rebound will bounce to the weak side. We must have players in position ready for the rebound to complete the defensive effort.

The difficulty in gaining weak-side rebounding position is that the weak-side players in our defense move to the midline of the court. On a shot their normal reaction is to turn and go directly to the hoop, thus giving up the weak-side rebound to their man. We must teach our players to fight this tendency and to move to position themselves on the weak side. We give our weak-side defenders two rules to follow upon seeing the shot released from the perimeter:

1. Turn away from the ball and run toward the weak side in an effort to beat your man to a spot outside the lane.
2. Make contact, box him out, and go for the ball.

To practice this specific skill we have set up the following drill. (See Diagram 3-44.)

The players line up on the baseline with the first two players stepping out—one as the offensive forward, the other as his

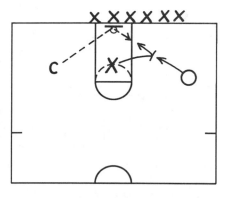

Diagram 3-44

defender. The coach stands on the opposite side of the court, with the ball. The offensive player drifts up and down his side of the court forcing the defender to move to maintain proper weak-side alignment on the midline of the court. On the coach's shot, the defender turns, beats his man to a spot, boxes him out, and goes for the ball. A successful defensive rebound releases this man to the end of the line. An offensive rebound results in one-on-one to the basket and a repeat of the drill.

Emphasize: Sprint to get position on the weak side, not under the basket; make contact, anticipate the weak-side bounce, and jump to the ball.

Perimeter box-out drill. This drill helps players master the skills needed to rebound from the check-and-go area and the weak side.

See Diagram 4-45. Four offensive players take their place around the perimeter. Four defenders then match up and take their proper positions as dictated by the location of the ball. The offensive players begin the drill by passing the ball around the perimeter and the defenders react on each movement of the ball by adjusting their defensive position to comply with our defensive rules. During this phase of the drill we allow the ball to go untouched through passing lanes even if it could be deflected or stolen by a defender. We are working toward maintaining proper defensive position and then rebounding out of this situation.

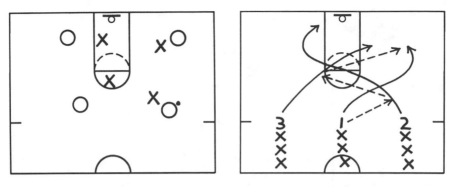

Diagram 3-45   Diagram 3-46

After an unspecified number of passes, one of the offensive players shoots the ball and the players go hard for the rebound. Strong-side players perform techniques that are used in the check-and-go area, while weak-side players follow the rules we have set up for weak-side rebounding. Regardless of the result—a defensive rebound, a made basket, an offensive rebound—the ball is tossed back out front and the drill restarted. After five shots, the defense runs a lap for every offensive rebound given up. The offensive group moves to defense and four new players enter as offensive players.

Emphasize: Anticipate a miss on every shot, go after the ball with two hands.

MULTIPURPOSE DEFENSIVE DRILLS

Three-man weave. Multipurpose offensive/defensive drill.

Most practices begin with warm-up drills in which players throw passes, shoot lay-ups, or work on other offensive skills. We use our share of these but have included in our repertoire of warm-up drills a defensive version of the three-man weave. Using this drill helps to convey to our players the importance of defense and accustoms them to playing defense right from the start of practice. (See Diagram 3-46.)

The players arrange themselves into three lines at half-court. The ball starts in the middle line in player 1's hand. Player

1 passes to 2 and goes behind, 2 passes to 3 and goes behind, and 3 feeds the ball back to 1 in the corner. What follows next is the execution of a defensive skill. The players then return to the back of the next line (rotate to the right).

First time through: Defender (3) plays the shooter (1). Player 3 follows his pass to 1 by moving toward him in an attempt to close him out. Player 1 receives the pass, takes one dribble, then goes up for the shot. Player 3 contests the shot, then works to gain inside position to prevent an offensive rebound. If the shot goes in or 2 or 3 get the rebound, the next group starts the drill with a second ball.

Second time through: Defender (3) forces the offensive player (1) baseline. Player 3 throws a lazy pass to 1 so that he can arrive in defensive position as 1 receives the pass. He is now covering the ball in the corner and has the responsibility of forcing the ball baseline where he has weak-side help (2). Player 1 takes the ball to the basket, and this group plays one-on-two basketball until 1 scores or the defense gets the ball.

Third time through: Defender (3) denies the flashing post (2). After 3 passes to 1, he assumes weak-side defensive position on 2. Player 1 holds the ball and looks to pass it to 2 as he flash cuts across the lane to the post area. Player 3 moves to beat this man to a spot and continues to move his feet to deny 2 the ball in the post area. Player 1 looks to get the ball inside to 2 (no lob passes) and must force a pass inside after five seconds go by. This portion of the drill ends when the offense scores or the defense gets the ball.

Fourth time through: Defender (3) boxes out weak-side player (2). After 3 passes to 1, he once again assumes weak-side defensive position on 2. On receiving the pass, 1 shoots, forcing 3 to perform a weak side box-out on 2. Play continues until the offense scores or 3 gets the ball.

Fifth time through ("Two-on-One"): After 3 passes the ball to 1, 1 and 2 become offensive players with 3 the defender in a two-on-one situation to the basket. Player 3 must protect the basket in this situation and may not give up an uncontested lay-up. He might step out at the ball and then quickly retreat in an attempt to have the ballhandler prematurely pick up his dribble, or he might try to draw the charge. We want this defender to do anything in his power to disrupt the offense while not giving up position near the basket. Play continues until the offense scores or the defense gets the ball.

Shell drill.   Ties all the fundamentals together and works on the team concept of defense.

See Diagram 3-47. Once all of the defensive fundamentals have been introduced and worked on by the players, we use the Shell Drill to help coordinate all of these defensive techniques into the team concept that we are striving for. This drill is set up as simply a four-on-four to the basket with the emphasis on defensive performance. We want the players to maintain proper position at all times as well as follow the eight rules that constitute the guts of this defense. Any error, whether physical or mental, is acknowledged and corrected on the spot. Good efforts and sound judgments are also recognized and are reinforced to encourage positive results.

To start this drill, the coach selects desirable match-ups as he chooses four offensive and four defensive players. These players take the court while the remaining players (usually four in number) go off to a side basket to shoot free throws. The ball is placed at the disposal of an offensive guard and the four-on-four action starts with the coach attentive and constantly monitoring the play. For motivational purposes, we have set up "bonuses"

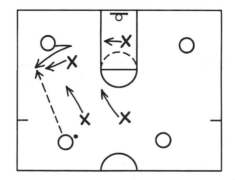

Diagram 3-47

that players can attain for outstanding defensive play during this drill. Any charge taken or dive on the floor to secure a loose ball constitutes an automatic bonus. Other notable defensive plays can also be judged by the coach as worthy of a bonus. These bonuses can be used later in practice to reduce the conditioning load for the entire squad. We allow players who have accumulated bonuses to shoot a free throw per bonus before any conditioning drill, with a made free throw resulting in a reduction or possible elimination of that drill. We have found that this reward system has helped to promote good defensive play and at the same time generated team spirit with the notion that individual benefits are shared by the entire team.

Variations of the shell drill: Normally we keep the same group of four on defense for seven minutes, then rotate the foul shooters to offense, and the offense to defense. The drill is run entirely at one basket with all rebounds, steals, baskets, etc., resulting in a stoppage of play and the ball being returned out front to the offense. After three rotations and twenty minutes of intense work, this drill has reached its limit of effectiveness and it is time to move on to something else. Occasionally, however, we change the rules of "Shell" to give it a fresh approach for our players. Some variations are:

1. **Make it—take it**. We set up our regular shell drill, only this time the two groups exchange roles every time the defense stops the offense. The offense has to "make it"—score a basket—in order to hold onto the basketball. We have included offensive rebounds and defensive fouls as reasons to keep possession. A defensive steal or rebound allows the defensive group to take over on offense.

2. **Four-on-four-on-four**. One group is chosen as defense, the next as offense, and the third to stand at half-court. The offensive group and the half-court group alternate turns going against the defense. The defensive group must perform a "triple play"—stop the offense three times in a row—in order to rotate out to midcourt. The offensive group that is the victim of the third straight stop takes over as the defensive group and tries for the "triple play" on the other two

groups. Any basket or offensive rebound by the offense, or foul by the defense, is a victory by the offense and pushes the defense back to zero. We have found that this variation, used on an intermediate basis, sparks a competitive nerve in our players that adds intensity to the drill.

3. **Perfection.** When we tell our players that we are going to run the "Shell Drill to Perfection," they know that all mistakes will be penalized in the form of laps. After each possession, the coach points out any mistake (didn't front low post, no weak-side box-out, reach in foul, etc.) and keeps a running total of mistakes. Outstanding plays (offensive foul, five-second deny on the ball, etc.) are ways that the defense can take laps off the total (at the coach's discretion, of course). At the end of a predetermined time or number of possessions, the defense "pays up" by running their laps while the next group rotates in to continue the drill.

4. **Transition shell.** Another way to change the face of this drill is to run it full court. On occasion we will tell the defense to "go" when they get the ball, thus adding transition to the objectives of this drill. Any time the defense steals or rebounds the ball we want them to push it down the court. This will force the offense to make a quick transition to defense, thus increasing our ability to stop teams that like to run. We make certain that the defense earns the ball in this drill. Any made basket or ball that goes out-of-bounds goes back out front to the offense.

5. **Five-on-four.** Five offensive players play against four defenders. The ball starts out front, and the offensive player farthest from the ball is left unguarded. The defensive players play by our defensive rules, with all defenders aware of the open man and ready to help out if he becomes a threat. Any time the ball is passed to this player, the nearest defender sprints out, calls "I've got ball," and closes him out, while the other defenders readjust to cover the players that are in the most advantageous positions. For the defense to be successful, the players must constantly move to cover open players and communicate to avoid confusion.

FOUR

DEVELOPING
THE FULL-COURT PRESS

All coaches have in their defensive inventory a system of full-court pressure that usually includes several different looks and strategies. Some coaches lean toward zone-based presses, others use the man-to-man as the basic structure. Most coaches eventually work both philosophies into their list of presses.

ADVANTAGES OF ZONE AND MAN-TO-MAN PRESSES

Zone pressing has become popular because it is easy to teach, and proper execution can reap big benefits for a ball club in a relatively short period of time. In zone presses, players are taught reactionary responsibilities and their movement is mostly calculated—based on what the offense predictably will do. Double teams are the catalyst in this defense, and this represents a gamble—but a gamble worth taking to many coaches. Man-to-man pressing, on the other hand, is a much more conservative approach. Each player matches up with a man and then prevents him from getting a pass or delays his progress if he has the ball. With defenders responsible for their own men and no double teams, there is little risk with this strategy. Little risk, however, provides little return (few turnovers), and the plan behind the man-to-man press is usually a long-range one: to wear down the opposition.

I have always been partial to the zone press philosophy. Double-team the ball, rotate the other three players to shut off passing lanes, and challenge the opposition to make quick, correct decisions. Any hesitation or miscalculation by the ballhandler and the offense is at the mercy of the defense. Turnovers are converted into quick baskets, close games turn into comfortable leads. With our already aggressive nature on defense, the zone press philosophy fits our style very nicely.

While developing my coaching ideals, I did a lot of experimenting with full-court zone pressure. We ran presses that trapped the first pass, others that trapped the second. Special presses were designed to drop to the hash mark before the trapping began, others to half-court. We toyed with the man-to-man press, but there wasn't enough going on with this defense and it was often shelved for future use and then forgotten. We preferred to live or die by the zone press.

After a measure of success, with some failures along the way, I sat down and analyzed the effectiveness of our pressure game. I came to the realization that where some teams were overwhelmed by our full-court zone pressure, others handled it with little trouble. Teams that passed well, for example, got the ball to the middle and tore us apart. Teams that relied on their point guard to dribble through pressure were feasted on by our press. Well-coached teams that ran disciplined patterns found the seams, while disorganized attacks found trouble. I was also aware of a problem of complication that existed within our pressure system. We ran at least two, sometimes as many as four different presses, and it was confusing to the players when and where to trap, when and where to rotate, etc. Our pressing game was in need of revision.

This revision began by carefully analyzing what was already in existence. I looked at all the presses that we ran, listed their strengths and weaknesses, and then established the following criteria as necessary components of a successful press:

1. There must be a double team on the ball.
2. It must be able to work against all press-breaking styles (passing/dribbling).
3. Forward passes, especially those to the middle, cannot be allowed.
4. A defender must always be kept deep to prevent any free lay-ups.
5. It should be consistent with our half-court philosophy.

INGREDIENTS FOR A SUCCESSFUL PRESS

Criterion 1: The Double Team

To make pressing worthwhile, the ball has to be double-teamed on every possession. Chances have to be taken to steal the ball each and every time the press is called. Minimizing the risk that is generated by this double team becomes the key to successful pressure.

Criterion 2: Adaptability to Press-breaking Styles

Teams attack pressure defense in a variety of ways. We have found success with the passing game against zone pressure and with clearing out and letting our point guard bring the ball upcourt when man-to-man pressure is applied. Quick passing versus zones moves the ball faster than defenders can rotate. Once the ball gets to the middle, all trapping angles are gone and the press is broken. Against man-to-man pressure—where there is more concern at shutting down passing lanes to all players—we don't look to pass. We get the ball into the hands of one of our guards and let him dribble up the floor. One defender is not going to stop even an average ballhandler.

Taking our press-breaking success into consideration, our press must be able to shut off all passing lanes while rotating to double team. We don't want dribblers or passers to beat us.

Criterion 3: Contesting Forward Passes

Forward passes hurt a press—passes to the middle kill it. There must always be a concern for players ahead of the ball. With man-to-man pressure, this objective is addressed when all defenders line up in ball-you-man positions. Passing lanes to teammates are shut off, but with no double team in effect we are not forcing the ballhandler to pass. With zone pressure, players guard men in their assigned area, then move to high-percentage passing areas when the ball is trapped. Offenses that find the seams between two defenders or overload one defender's area often have success passing through the press.

So in meeting this objective, a dilemma exists. Man-to-man pressure exerts minimum, almost ineffective, pressure on the ball yet provides the perfect off-the-ball coverage. Zone pressure puts forth maximum pressure on the ball (the double team), yet shows a weakness in shutting off passing lanes to teammates.

Criterion 4: No Free Lay-ups

The press isn't going to force a turnover every time it is used—this is a fact we all must face up to. But as long as we don't foul or give up an easy lay-up, this pressure has worked to wear down the opposition to a degree. Repeated use will cause added wear and tear. Fouling usually results from overaggressiveness; easy lay-ups generally result from bad decisions that lead to poor positioning.

Where full-court zone pressure takes into account always rotating a defender deep, positioning in man-to-man pressure is totally reliant on the offensive set-up. Most press-breakers employ a deep offensive player so his defender becomes the deep man or "safety valve" in the press. Press-breaking schemes that bring all five players into the back court leave the man-to-man defense susceptible to down-the-floor cuts that could lead to free lay-ups. Adjustments can be made to drop players back, but at the expense of weakening the press.

Criterion 5: Compatible With Half-Court Philosophy

We have made a commitment to run the team man-to-man as our half-court defense. To lessen the complexity of our overall defensive system, it would behoove us to structure our full-court attack around the same principles. If combining the strengths of the man-to-man and zone defenses worked to develop a comprehensive defense that was right for us at the half-court level, then why not try the same plan for full-court pressure. We have done just that and are pleased with the results.

BENEFITS OF A PRESSING DEFENSE

Drawing strengths from our zone and man-to-man presses, we have developed what we feel is a very effective press. Our players have confidence that we can press anyone, so pressing has now become a part of every game plan that we prepare. Teams that are going to play us must prepare for full-court pressure, because they are sure to see a varying amount in their game against us. Beyond the steals and turnovers that represent the obvious advantages, our pressing philosophy has paid off with these additional seven dividends.

Tough Defense to Play Against

The press makes a team play against 84 feet of defense rather than 20 feet–25 feet. Instead of dribbling the ball down the court unchallenged, teams must now use strategy, concentration, and energy to advance the ball to an area where they can start their offense. Teams in poor condition will fall prey to this defense and will be more prone to turnovers as the game wears on. Even teams in good shape will eventually feel the effects of a constant press. Also, we have long felt that kids don't develop ballhandling skills to the degree they should and pressing is a good way to expose this weakness.

Speeds Up the Tempo of the Game

One of my players once asked me, "What's tempo, Coach?" It seems like I've added this word to my basketball vocabulary without explaining it to my players. Tempo is the speed at which a team can effectively control their play. Some teams play better at a slow pace, others shine when the pace is quickened. The press speeds up the pace of the game, making it difficult for those teams who are most efficient at a lesser speed. Pressing strategies may have to vary for teams that prefer a fast tempo.

Gives You a Chance to Win Every Game You Play

As we alluded to before, relying on the offense to win games is a dangerous practice. Some nights, things just don't go well. It is on these nights that aggressive full-court defense can be just the move to get things going. I can think of games in which we had fallen way behind and then came back to win—it was the press that led the charge. In a sport that is full of momentum swings, it is necessary to have the ability to push momentum in the right direction. Pressing is our catalyst to get this done.

Nullifies a Size Disadvantage

For those teams without the true "big man" or size to match up underneath with their opponents, the press is a great equalizer. To break the press, teams must bring their forwards and center out away from the basket. These players are now in areas where quickness can neutralize size.

We tell our players that the good post player won't hurt us if he doesn't get the ball down low. We gear our team man-to-man defense around accomplishing this—the press helps us to meet this objective as well.

Leads to a Press "Reputation"

We have used the press so much in the last few years that we have developed a reputation of being a pressing team. Opponents know that they will be pressed at some time during their game with us. It might be a lot or just for a few possessions, but they will see our press. Because of this, I know that teams have to spend practice time getting ready for the full-court press, and this is at the expense of drills or preparations that would normally be done to stop our offense. Coaches are concerned when their teams come up against pressing opponents.

Also, being a pressing team, we don't often see the press used against us. I have had a couple of teams that were very "pressable," but opposing coaches looked at our pressing "reputation" and chose to back off. Our vulnerability wasn't usually exposed until those moments of desperation when our opponents fell behind, were forced to press, and then saw that our "reputation" had exceeded their expectations.

Works Eight or Nine Players into the Action

An uptempo, baseline-to-baseline game is going to take more than five players to carry out. The pressing defense, more than any other, calls for a team effort. Periodic substitutions must be made to keep the players fresh and the press effective. To keep pace with the game, opponents must substitute as well. If this isn't common practice for them, our defensive pressure will prey on either the weariness of their starters or the inexperience of their substitutes.

Developing depth helps us not only physically, but mentally as well. Teams that use their bench generally have more team spirit than those that go the distance with the starting five.

Teaches Players How to Beat the Press

We work on our press every day in practice. Not only do our skills to press improve, but our skills to break the press do as well. Our players go against so much full-court pressure in practice that they are not at all alarmed when facing this type of pressure in games. And where our press is a man-to-man type with zone rotations and traps, we gain valuable experience going against both man-to-man and zone presses that we see during the season.

PRESSING CONCERNS

After listing all that the press can do for a team, it is important to expose its limitations as well. I've already mentioned the assets that a press can bring to a team, now I'm going to discuss its liabilities. The wise coach must investigate both sides before deciding whether or not to invest in the pressing defense. There are four major concerns that result from the pressing game.

It Is Tiring

Plain and simple, pressing is hard work. The amount of pressing a team can do in a game relies heavily on its depth. It would be unrealistic for a coach to demand that his "iron five" press effectively if they are on the court for the entire game. For teams with little depth, pressing may wear out the starters and negate any advantage they may have over their opponents. For teams with depth (eight or nine players the coach feels confident putting into the game), this liability turns into an asset when the opposition wears down.

Foul Trouble

We tell our players that they must be aggressive while pressing. When they foul, we tell them that they are "overaggressive." There is a fine line between the two. No matter what the match-ups are, with a press that rotates and goes after the ball a certain amount of fouling is to be expected. I have never coached a team that didn't outfoul the opposition throughout the course of the season. If I had, I'm sure that I would have told them that they weren't aggressive enough. Once again, to overcome this liability, the coach must have confidence in his bench.

Easy Baskets

No matter how much time we spend on trying to prevent this, easy baskets sometimes result from full-court pressure. We tell our players to gamble, to anticipate—and wrong decisions on defense or great decisions on offense can lead to unchallenged hoops. The coach must be patient, however, and not take the press off every time a lay-up occurs.

He must prepare for occasional breakdowns and teach his players how to adjust.

One Weak Defender

Sometimes there is a player on the team who just can't press. He may be an important cog in the offensive machine, but a defensive malfunction. Pressing is a team game, and one weak defender could possibly render the full-court effort useless. Realistically, there are some lineups that a coach puts on the floor that simply can't press.

After weighing the plusses and minuses of pressing, this type of defense *can* be a benefit to your program. I do not profess nor do I practice the idea that teams should press 32 minutes per game, every game; but the press can be used to gain an advantage at some time during the course of each contest.

THE COACH'S COMMITMENT

To find success, the pressing defense takes a total commitment on behalf of the coach and players. Whether he intends to use the press exclusively or occasionally, the coach must "sell the press" to his players. He must be able to convince them of the positive returns that the press can yield. We sell the press to our players by explaining to them that it represents our commitment to win. I vow to my teams each year that we will work harder than any opponent and be best prepared to play to win each and every time we take the floor. Preparing my teams to press is one way to "practice what I preach."

The pressing defense offers both an exciting and a calculating strategy. The end-to-end pressure livens up the action and generates excitement, and at the same time this tactic serves to wear on the opponents' minds. They know that the defense will always be there and this physical (and mental) pressure will eventually lead to mental mistakes, physical mistakes, or a departure from the game plan. Even if the press isn't stealing the ball, it is still working to wear down the opponent.

THE PLAYERS' COMMITMENT

The coach prepares the players—the players get the job done. For the press to work, the players must commit: (1) effort to the process, (2) persistence for its success, and (3) confidence in their teammates. The full-court press is a tough defense to play. Energy has to be expended by all teammates throughout the opponents' possession, all over the court. There are times the press is going to get beaten—no press that I know of steals the ball every time. But our players have got to bounce back and try just as hard the next time. I have already mentioned that the press is a gamble. When we press we want our players to outhustle and outguess the offense. We demand the outhustle part—we hope that we can outguess them. If the guess is wrong and the press is beaten, defenders are going to cover for each other until they all have sprinted back into the play.

The team concept that we rely on so heavily in our half-court defense is a necessary ingredient for our full-court defense as well.

FIVE

TEACHING
THE FULL-COURT PRESS

We call our press "55" (five-on-five full-court) and it is, more or less, an extension of our half-court defense. Like the team man-to-man, "55" combines man-to-man skills with zone strategy to get maximum coverage on and off the ball. Not only have we come up with a very effective press, but its basic principles are similar to those used in our basic half-court team man-to-man. Because of this, our players view our half-court and full-court defenses as a total defensive package rather than as separate entities.

BASIC PREMISE OF "55"

Start in a man-to-man alignment to account for all players and limit the passing game. The man-to-man continues as long as the ball stays off the floor—we cannot allow teams to pass through our press. Once the ball is dribbled, the defender on the ball turns the dribbler, a teammate moves to double the ball, and the other three players rotate to shut off logical passing lanes. From the first dribble on, there is no set assignment, and defensive players may end up guarding any one of the offensive players.

THE PHASES OF THE PRESS

To best explain press responsibilities to our players, we have broken the press down into five phases. Within each phase, rules have been established that the players must carry out until the press moves on to the next stage. By spending time to break down each phase, the entire press is understood by all players.

The five phases of our press are:

1. Ball is held out-of-bounds.
2. Inbounds pass is thrown.
3. First dribble is made.
4. Initial double team is broken.
5. Press is beaten.

Listing the phases in this manner does give a somewhat pessimistic view of our chances to succeed while pressing. Listing "initial double team is broken" and "press is beaten" as phases of our press doesn't necessarily mean that we expect this to happen, only that we are prepared in the event that it does. Quite frankly, we feel that we can steal the ball or force a turnover in any one of the five phases.

AN EXPLANATION OF THE FIVE PHASES

The need to teach all the players all the press responsibilities is of the utmost importance. This defense is totally dependent on a team effort. If even one player gets caught out of position in any one of the five phases, the press has little chance of succeeding.

Phase 1: Ball Is Held Out-of-Bounds

The press begins with a man-to-man match-up—we want to deny the inbound pass as well as we can.

We can set up our press after made field goals or anytime the ball is awarded by the officials to our opponents anywhere along the baseline. For the latter, we will have ample time to set up, but for the former, our players must realize that the press starts when the ball enters the basket, not when the opposition steps out-of-bounds to throw it in. As the ball falls through the net, our players must find their men and get to a position ready to implement the press. From the moment our opponents touch the ball we want them to see and feel pressure. During this phase our players have the following responsibilities depending on where their assignment lines up.

On the ball. Toes near the baseline, hands in the air. We play this man slightly toward the inside to encourage passes to the outside and away from the middle. The weight is on the balls of the feet, and the knees are slightly flexed to react to any baseline running that can occur after a basket or to a long pass to which the defender must jump and reach in an effort to deflect the ball. This player must be active, giving the offense the message that they are in for trouble. We cannot allow this player to half-heartedly shadow the inbounds passer—this sets a poor tone for the defense and gives the offense a good chance at getting the ball where we don't want it to go.

One pass away. One pass away, by our definition, is any player who lines up on or below the foul line extended or who is in a position where a simple cut will bring him to this area (see Diagram 5-1). Players just beyond this area standing still or moving toward the ball are considered "one pass away."

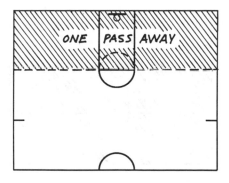

Diagram 5-1

Defenders in this area are in a deny position, forcing the pass to be thrown over their head or into the deep corner. Their stance is the very same denial stance used in the team man-to-man: ball-you-man, base wide, knees bent, foot nearer ball up, and inside arm extended into the passing lane. A major concern here is that the ball is not received in the middle of the court. We want the defenders in this area to take chances to steal the ball ("Be aggressive!"), but not at the expense of allowing the ball in the middle. Even if a steal is not made, forcing the ball to be thrown in to a player not in the middle sets up the second phase of our press. The wider the player is forced, the better our chances are going to be to effectively trap the ball. Passes inbounded to the middle have us looking to Phase 5 (Recovery) without a really good chance of applying further pressure.

Two passes away. We define "two passes away" as any player who is beyond the 28-foot hash mark (see Diagram 5-2) or any player in the "median strip" (area from the foul line to the hash mark) who is moving downcourt. Players in the "median strip" standing still or moving toward the ball are considered "one pass away" and are covered accordingly.

During the initial phase of the press while the ball is being held out-of-bounds by our opponents, the defender in the "two

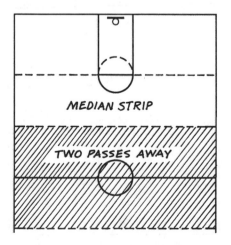

Diagram 5-2

passes away" area has a twofold responsibility. First, he must position himself so that his man doesn't receive the inbounds pass, and second, he must be ready to help on any passes lobbed over defenders in the "one pass away" area.

In defending his man from receiving the inbounds pass, this player must assume a stance similar to the weak-side stance used in the half-court team man-to-man. He must open up to the ball with his back to the middle. His hands should likewise be used: one to point to the ball and the other toward his man to keep him constantly informed of the location of both. If his man cuts deep to the basket for the "home run pass," he must be in a position where he can react to this move and deny this player access to the ball. The same applies if his man cuts to the ball—the defender "two passes away" must stay alert. As a general rule, we tell this defender that the farther away his man is to the ball, the more distance he can allow between himself and his man.

The second concern for this player is to help his teammates playing on the front line. If they are doing a good job of denying the inbounds pass, their men may choose to cut deep to get open. Our defenders in the "two passes away" area must be ready to step in and prevent this ploy used by the offense in hopes of opening up for a pass.

A look at our Phase 1 coverage can be found in Diagram 5-3. We tell our back-line defenders on the press to key off the inbounds passer. He has only five seconds to inbound the ball, so his eyes and body movement will usually forecast where his pass will go. Gaining only a slight advantage on this pass may be the difference between stealing or getting a piece of the ball and getting beat for a clean lay-up. We encourage our players to gamble—we teach them to make intelligent bets.

Reading the eyes is a natural part of our defensive system and one that our players should be familiar with. The inbounds passer's eyes almost always lead to the target. Reading body movement is something that must be ingrained into our players. How far the passer cocks the ball back, for example, may be an indication of how far he intends to throw the pass. We have found that inbounds passers with a stance square to the baseline (both toes pointing forward) almost always throw a short pass into the "one pass away" area. When this passer turns so that one foot is

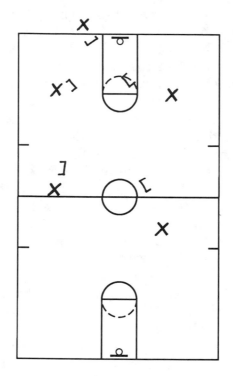

Diagram 5-3

in front of the other and the toes point to the side, chances are he is preparing to throw long. With only five seconds and not a lot of time to dance around, our players have had a lot of success reading feet.

Teaching Point: Never let the opponent beat you the same way twice.

Any time the press is beaten as a result of the inbounds pass, we tell our players to adjust during the next possession to make the offense do something different. For example, if the first pass came into the lane, we will tell our defenders in the "one pass away" area to pay less attention denying the ball to their men and more emphasis on forcing them to go wide to receive it ("Let him get it wide"). If we are beaten by the "home run" pass, back-line players have to back up a bit the next time. This may lessen front-line support but it will force the offense to do something different on their next possession to beat the pressure.

It is important for our players to realize that Phase 1 is but one part of "55." We don't have to make the steal in this stage for our press to work, but we do have to force the offense to areas (specifically the corners) that are beneficial for what we want to do.

Phase 2: Inbounds Pass Is Thrown

We stay with the man-to-man match-up. Our goal now is to get the offense to dribble the ball—we can't leave any passing lanes open.

If we have done our job during Phase 1, the offense will only be able to get the ball to a guard cutting toward the sideline. When this pass is in the air, all defenders will move to adjust their positions so that they remain between the ball and their men (ball-you-man). Once the ball is caught, our defenders must deny any penetrating pass down the floor, especially to the middle (see Diagram 5-4). We want the offense to put the ball on the floor so that we can move onto Phase 3. To accomplish this, our players must adhere to the following individual responsibilities.

Player guarding the ballhandler. This man is guarded similarly to how he would be defended in the team man-to-man. The defender plays this man half a step to the middle with the inside foot up forcing any dribble to be toward the sideline. He is close enough to reach out and touch his man and is ready to react to deflect any pass that might be thrown.

If this player should pass the ball laterally, the defender steps to the ball to maintain a ball-you-man relationship. If a penetrating (downcourt) pass is thrown, this defender must turn and sprint to the level of the ball. He is looking to close off passing lanes or double-team the ball—whatever the situation calls for.

Defenders off the ball. Players off the ball in this phase follow the rules that have already been established in the team man-to-man. The defender of any player behind the play (usually the player whose man took the ball out-of-bounds) will drop to the level of

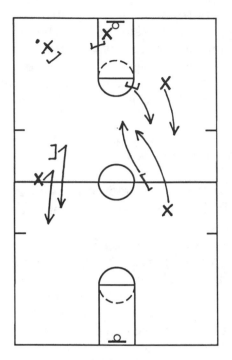

Diagram 5-4

the ball to help support any dribble penetration by the offense. As
in our half-court defense, we will allow teams to pass backward
during this phase of our press. Defenders of weak-side players
abide by the team man-to-man rules as well. By forcing the
inbound pass to be thrown in wide of the middle, we have helped
ourselves by establishing a strong side and a weak side. It is
important to note that we want these defenders to sag *toward* the
middle but not *to* the middle. These players must be ready to help,
but not at the expense of having their men open up for a lob pass
over the top. Any cut to the middle of the court must be defended
as if it were a flash cut into the lane—penetrating passes to the
middle may never be allowed. Players guarding strong-side players ahead of the ball must position themselves to prevent any pass
from the ballhandler to their men. Defenders of "deep" men, or
players two passes ahead of the ball, will sag the farthest off their
men and look to help on any long passes that are thrown.

Phase 3: First Dribble Is Made

If we have been successful through the first two stages of our press, the ball will be in a guard's hands wide of the lane with all passing lanes to teammates closed off. His next option is to dribble the ball, which triggers our rotation system to go into effect (see Diagram 5-5).

Man on-the-ball. He has already assumed a defensive stance forcing the ball to the sideline. Now he must react immediately when the ballhandler starts his dribble in that direction. This defender must now sprint beside his man, beat him to a spot, and then step in front to force him to turn (preferably with a reverse dribble). At this point he should receive help from a teammate to trap this man. We want to make this turn as quickly as possible, but insist that this defender clearly beats his man to a spot and doesn't rub or bump him to make the turn, causing a needless foul

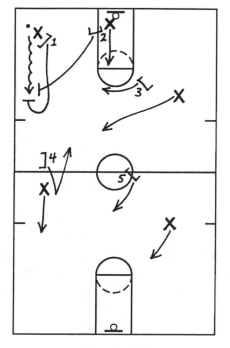

Diagram 5-5

in the process. The "turning limit" on our press is the hash mark in the forecourt, leaving this defender with over 50 feet to turn his man and little excuse for failing to do so.

We prefer that the ballhandler start his dribble toward the sideline, but if his first dribble is toward the middle, we will attempt a double team and rotation out of this situation as well.

The "trapper." All press responsibilities in "55" are predicated on player position when the first dribble is started. The defender nearest the ballhandler to the middle of the court becomes the "trapper." This will most likely be the player guarding the in-bounds passer (defender 2 in Diagram 5-5); but on occasion when this man passes and goes through, the trapper will then become the weak-side guard (defender 3 in Diagram 5-5).

On the dribble, the trapper leaves his man and sprints to double-team the dribbler. If all is going according to plan (dribble up the sideline with a reverse dribble on the turn), this player should be ready to steal the ball on the reverse dribble. If the dribbler is successful in picking up his dribble, these two defenders step up to trap this man to prevent him from finding the "seams" in our press.

If the initial dribble is toward the middle, this player still moves to trap, but is ready to help and recover to his man (Phase 4) as this would be a logical pass for the trapped dribbler.

The trap: Trapping a player who has used up his dribble sets up an advantage to the defense. Not only has it eliminated half of this player's options to escape, but it also breeds a sense of panic in the offense that often leads to rushed mistakes. So once we have our opponents trapped, we want to take full advantage. We tell our players that when they are involved in a trapping situation, they must apply maximum pressure on denying the offensive player vision of the court. This is best done by raising the arms straight up and mirroring any ball movement with the hands. These defenders should maintain a base slightly wider than their shoulders with slight flexion in the knees and weight on the balls of the feet to react to any pivoting that might be done by their opponent to establish a passing lane.

We are looking to deflect passes and steal the ball out of this situation, but we must continually caution our players not to be overaggressive and waste fouls when trapping the ball. If, at the least, we force any pass that is thrown to be lobbed, we will have time to recover before it is received, and our pressure has given us a chance at forcing a turnover without giving up anything in return. Traps generally grow in effectiveness as the game wears on.

The "third man." When the rotation begins and the trapper leaves his man to trap the ball, his man becomes a logical target for the ball-handler. Our "third man" takes this option away. The third man in our press is the next player on the weak side or in the middle once the trapper has left (defender 3 in Diagram 5-5). On the dribble, he moves to an area where he can intercept passes that are thrown back to the middle.

Players who anticipate well have a lot of success at this position. Dribblers who are trapped have limited options, and if our third man is aware of all the options, he can think along with the passer and outguess him for a steal. Even when this defender is unsuccessful at picking off a pass, if he can force a lateral or backward pass, we are in good shape to institute Phase 4 with the ten-second count now starting to weigh on our opponents' minds.

The "stealer." With two players converging to trap the ball and a third moving down to close off the passing lane to the middle, this leaves two defenders and two more responsibilities. The player whose man is farthest down the court is designated the "deep man." The remaining player is the "stealer." If a situation arises where both players are equally deep, the weak-side defender becomes the "deep man."

The stealer uses Phase 1 and Phase 2 to deny his man and to assess the situation to determine whether or not he is the deep man. Seeing a teammate farther back, he moves to a position to steal the ball once a dribble is made. By the nature of press-breakers, this player will be on the strong side or in the middle most of the time. We have already rotated two players (the trapper and third man) from the weak side; few teams would have yet another player in the backcourt on the weak side. Our stealer will usually be the player guarding the strong-side forward located near half-court (Defender 4 in Diagram 5-5).

On the dribble that initiates Phase 3, the stealer must continue to close off the passing lane to his man. His man is downcourt, probably in the line of sight of the dribbler, and presents a logical target for a pressured ballhandler. Once the ball is trapped, the stealer then moves to the middle, but remains close enough to his man to intercept any lob pass thrown in his direction. We don't want this player to be afraid to take chances. If he reads in the passer's eyes or by the way he is pivoting that the pass is going to the middle—go for it! If the offensive player in turn makes a good play to get it to his man at half-court, at best the offense has a two-on-one break with two forwards handling the ball. We just tell this player not to make the same judgmental mistake twice in a row. Remember: Never let the opponent beat you the same way twice.

The stealer should never be part of the original double team. If it should happen that the dribbler beats his defender up the sideline, it might seem natural that the half-court defender (either the stealer or the deep man) should step in, stop the ball, and create a double team with the dribbler's defender. We, in fact, used this in the infancy stages of this press until we realized what a low-percentage move it was with our rotation set up as it is. We found that whenever the half-court defender moved up to stop the dribbler: (1) the dribbler, a guard, used his full head of steam to go right by our forward, or (2) the dribbler flipped the ball over the defender's head to his man creating a two-on-one or three-on-one break. Only on rare occasions did the offense not end up with a fast break opportunity.

We have since revamped our rules and now demand that the original dribbler's defender turns his man or we have no double team. We now allow this player all the way to the front-court hash mark to execute this turn. If the ball comes up the sideline, half-court defenders may hedge (jab step then retreat) to help the dribbler's defender, but we don't want to challenge the dribbler with a backline defender at this point. If it is obvious that we are not going to get a turn, we move quickly to Phase 5, and all five defenders recover to the basket.

The "deep man." One of our basic principles when pressing is not to give up free lay-ups. With this in mind, we are always concerned with designating a player with deep responsibility who will be there to guard the basket even when all else fails in our pressing effort.

The "deep man" in the probable scenerio that was depicted in Diagram 5-5 is Defender 5. Press-breakers who send a player deep make this decision an easy one. Offenses that send two players equally deep (both to half-court) demand that our players have an awareness of the situation and a grasp of the rules of our press. We don't want to end up with two players who think they are each the deep man or, even worse, two players who think they are each the stealer and then both cheat upcourt.

With many press-breakers, the deep man is the weak-side defender at half-court. If this man should cut to the middle toward the ball before it is dribbled, then responsibilities change and any defender left behind becomes the deep man. Once the ball is dribbled, we are locked into our responsibilities until the ball-handler: (1) passes the ball, or (2) beats the double team. At this point we reassess the situation and move on to a new phase.

The deep man plays as deep as he needs to prevent any pass from the ballhandler to the deepest offensive player (usually his man). The farther he is from the ball, the more space he can allow between himself and his man, putting himself in a position where he will be able to steal a lobbed or deflected pass. This man is the last line of defense, however, and must make high-percentaged decisions. We want him going after passes that he knows he can get to—we don't want this player gambling and getting caught out of position.

If the press is broken, the deep man must retreat to the basket to not allow any free attempt to score. Anything that he can do to interrupt the progress of the offense will allow his teammates more time to recover and to get back into the play. But he cannot foul. We would rather give up two points over a stationary body and outstretched arms than having our deep man get in foul trouble trying to block every shot in sight.

Teaching point: On the first dribble, players must move when the ball leaves the dribbler's hands—not when it hits the floor. We must do all that we can to limit the transition time between the man-to-man and zone trapping phases of our press.

Phase 4: Initial Double Team Is Broken

Let's be realistic—we are not going to steal the ball every time we double-team the dribbler. But we want to make provisions to continue the pressure even when the initial double team is broken. Many presses limit their pressure to a single double team. Once that is broken, the press is considered beaten and the defenders all recover to the other end of the court. We want to keep the pressure on and consider ourselves still in "55" until the ball passes the hash mark in the front court or there is no resistance to allowing this to happen. Only at this point will we move to the recovery phase of the press.

When we rotate to double-team the ball we are taking chances, no question about it. Two players on the ball leave three defenders to cover four players. Teams will find open men to pass to out of the original double team no matter how well our off-the-ball players anticipate. Any time a successful pass is made out of this double team we want: (1) the defender nearest to the receiver (either the third man or the stealer) to challenge the ball, force the dribble toward the sideline, then turn him into a second double team; and (2) all other defenders stepping to the ball, with the nearest defender becoming the trapper and the others looking to pick off passes.

It is essential that the two players involved in the original double team react to this pass by quickly moving toward the receiver. In most cases, these two players will become the trapper and third man on the second double team. On occasion, when the stealer gets involved in the second double team, one of our defenders recovering to the ball will take over his responsibilities. One thing remains constant with each possession: once a player has been determined to be the deep man he continues in that role throughout the pressing effort, cheating up only when he knows that he can steal the ball.

Situation 1: Pass back to the inbounds passer. See Diagram 5-6. Defender 1 turns his man and double teams him with Defender

2. Defender 3 steps down as the third man while Defender 4 becomes the stealer and Defender 5 the deep man. One pass that might be made is back to the inbound passer. If Defender 3 successfully anticipates this pass, he steps in, steals it, and lays it in. If the pass is completed, however, our press continues with Defender 3 challenging the receiver and forcing him to put the ball on the floor. We want this player to feel immediate pressure so he won't have time to survey the floor and look for a possible pass. We want him to feel that he has to beat the pressure by dribbling to create an opening. If he heads toward the strong side, he will dribble right into another trap. Most logically, this player will dribble toward the weak side with Defender 3 pursuing, catching, then turning. Defenders 1 and 2, having reacted to the pass and dribble, are moving toward the ballhandler. Defender 2 is a little closer and so he takes over as the trapper; 1 peels off to the middle looking for a player to cover. Defender 4 retreats and

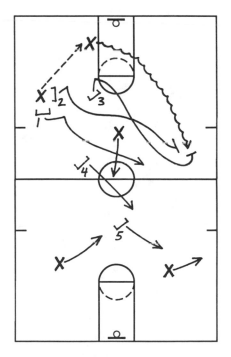

Diagram 5-6

searches for a downcourt player to cover, while Defender 5 moves back to protect the basket.

Any pass out of this second double team is reacted to in the same way—the defender nearest the receiver attacks the ball and forces it wide, the next closest defender becomes the trapper, and the others look to steal any pass. This continues until the ball crosses the hash mark in the forecourt or is being advanced with no resistance. At this point we take the man closest to us and play our team man-to-man defense.

Situation 2: Pass to half-court.   See Diagram 5-7. Defenders 1 and 2 double-team the dribbler. Defender 3 steps down as the third man, Defender 4 assumes the role of the stealer, and Defender 5 is the deep man. Another pass possibility is the strong-side pass down the line to a teammate at half-court. Once again, we would like our defender in this area (the stealer in this case) to read this

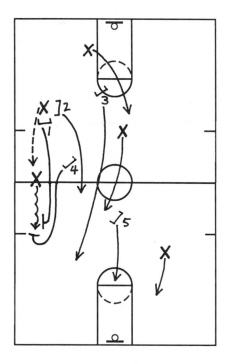

Diagram 5-7

pass being thrown and then step in and steal it, but we realize that there will be times when this pass is successful.

On those occasions, the defender closest to the ball—never the deep man, however—attacks the ball, forces him to put it on the floor, and attempts to turn the dribbler before the hash mark is reached. In the action shown by Diagram 5-7, Defender 4 is closest to the receiver and, assuming he has moved while the pass was in the air, he should be in good position to ride this man wide and turn him before the hash mark. Defenders 1 and 2 should also have reacted to the pass downcourt by turning and sprinting in its direction. The man closest to the receiver (Defender 1 in this case) becomes the trapper while Defender 2 looks for possible passing options in the middle. Defender 3 moves downcourt on the pass to half-court, sees the stealer on the ball, and sprints by to take his place downcourt. The deep man retreats to protect the basket. Any penetration beyond the hash mark or successful pass to the middle in the front court ends our pressing effort and the rules of the team man-to-man take over.

Situation 3: Pass to the middle.   See Diagram 5-8. Defenders 1 and 2 double-team the ball, Defender 3 is once again the third man, Defender 4 is the stealer, and Defender 5 is the deep man. Teams are coached to get the ball into the middle against the press, and occasionally they are successful against us. This certainly puts us at a disadvantage, but we do not consider our press broken until the ball is in the middle over half-court or beyond the hash mark on either side.

As the ball is in flight toward the middle, the defender nearest to the receiver (most likely the stealer) attacks the ball, causes the man to dribble, forces the dribbler wide of the middle, then turns him before the hash mark. All other defenders have reacted to the pass to the middle by moving in that direction. The next nearest defender (the third man in Diagram 5-8) assumes the role of the trapper, and the other defenders fill in where they see offensive options.

In all of our scenerios we have assumed that the player with the ball will dribble away from pressure toward the weak side. If he should, for some reason, dribble toward the traffic on the strong side, the nearest two players stop the dribble and double

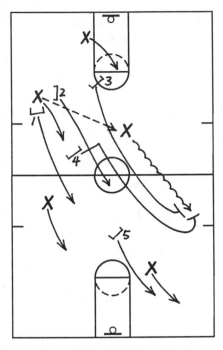

Diagram 5-8

the ball, while the rest of the defenders move to logical passing outlets.

We have found this phase to be a very productive one for our press. Many teams breathe a sigh of relief when they escape the original double team because, with most presses, that is the extent of pressure exerted on any one possession. Capturing them in a second double team often catches them off guard, unprepared, and with their pressbreaking pattern in disarray.

Phase 5: Recovery

Knowing that "55" is a gamble and that teams are going to beat our pressure, we have made provisions for dealing with this situation. Our basic principle during this phase is "No free lay-ups," but our players realize that all-out hustle may result in a steal or forced turnover even at this late stage of the press. During the course of any game we give up our share of two-on-one and three-on-two breaks. But, by the nature of our press, the offense usually has the ball in a forward's hands with the guards happy to have got it by our pressure. Forwards leading the fast break do not necessarily create an advantage for the offense. Our players who sprint back can catch the fast break to poke the ball away from behind, or step in to steal predictable passes to the wings. At the least, their impending presence can force a rushed shot at the basket which marks yet another victory for the press.

We consider the recovery phase of our press in effect when the ball is over half-court in the middle, beyond the hash mark on either side, or in a position where an opportunity to stop or turn the ball no longer exists. At this point all defenders spring back to the lane to help the deep man prevent an easy shot. If the deep man is back alone, he stays near the basket and does his best to slow down the offensive effort without leaving the lane. If, however, there are at least two defenders between the ball and the basket, one defender must slow the dribbler (we tell him to "Stop the ball!"), while a second protects the basket and waits for recovery help.

It is important that we utilize communication skills during this phase. We are in a transition situation and must pick up our men quickly to prevent easy scoring opportunities. This can only be accomplished through hustling down the court all the way to the lane and then calling out, "I've got ball," "I've got twenty-four," etc., so that all the offensive players are accounted for and none end up all alone near the basket.

SPECIAL PRESSBREAKERS THAT NECESSITATE ADJUSTMENT

One problem that our press has presented to our opponents is for them to figure out what type of defense we are in. Is it man-to-man? It certainly starts out that way. Is it a match-up zone? With all those rotations this must certainly be the case. As a result, teams run zone pressbreakers against us (very ineffective), man-to-man pressbreakers (effective at times), and special pressbreakers that cause us to adjust. Most situations can be dealt with by simply applying the pressing rules—force the dribble, turn the ball, double team, rotate, etc.—with each player assuming the role that is dictated to him by his position on the court.

There are four situations that have given us difficulty over the years. We have resolved three of them, and the fourth motivated us to give our press a "face-lift."

Inbounds Passer Goes Through

See Diagram 5-9. Most teams leave their inbounds passer behind the ball as a safety valve. Occasionally they will run this player through the middle in hopes of getting him open for a quick return pass on the go. By applying our rules, however, this man should not open up. There has yet to be a dribble, so the inbounds passer's defender should have stepped to the ball, seen his man going through, and then taken an inside denial route to deny his man access to the ball.

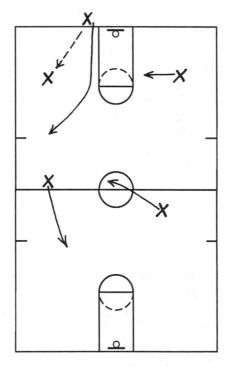

Diagram 5-9

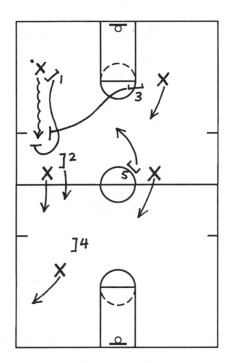

Diagram 5-10

See Diagram 5-10. As soon as this defender gets ahead of the ball, he is no longer the trapper once the ball is dribbled. This responsibility now falls into the hands of the next nearest defender on the weak side, Defender 3 (normally the third man). On the dribble, he moves to trap while the next weak-side defender (Defender 5 in this case) sprints down to take over the third man role. Defender 2 becomes the stealer and Defender 4 retreats as the deep man. From this point on we conduct our press as we would under normal circumstances.

The "Dreaded 1-4"

See Diagram 5-11. This pressbreaking alignment presents a problem to any man-to-man type press (so much, in fact, that we use it ourselves). Teams that aggressively deny the ball are wide open for a backdoor cut and breakaway lay-up. After years of trial

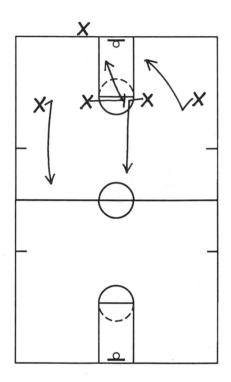

Diagram 5-11

and error (man on the inbounds passer plays deep, weak-side wing's defender plays deep, etc.), we have finally resolved a way to play this alignment that is consistent with our pressing rules (Diagram 5-12).

All five defenders line up on their men, but we now allow the first pass to come in with minimum resistance. We compromise our Phase 1 denial by playing behind the wings, allowing them an easy pass from the inbounds passer, but by aggressively playing the middle two players (most likely the guards) from cutting to the ball and getting it in the middle. By doing this, we have allowed a virtually uncontested pass-in (usually to a forward), but have our defenders on the wings ready to help out on any backdoor cut by any player. If one of the middle players should cut deep, a wing defender will pick him up and switch men with this player's defender. We now have a forward as our potential

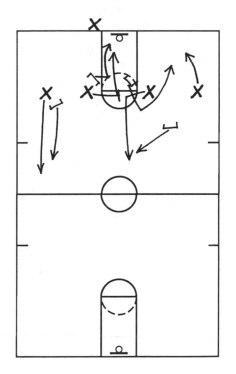

Diagram 5-12

deep man and a guard defending a player in an area that will most likely make him the trapper or third man.

Once the ball is dribbled, we adhere strictly to our pressing rules with the man on the ball forcing it wide and turning the dribbler, the next man on the weak side becoming the trapper, and the other three players adjusting to their roles as dictated by their location on the court.

The Clear-out

See Diagram 5-13. One way to eliminate the double team, many teams figure, is to clear out the area, leaving no other defenders around to double the ball. Good thought—bad strategy. We are still going to apply our rules, only this time the ballhandler won't have anybody to pass to.

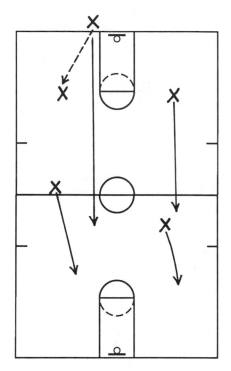

Diagram 5-13

While the ballhandler waits for his teammates to clear, his defender realizes that it is just him and his man in the immediate area. Help isn't as close as it usually is, so instead of quickly turning his man, he is more concerned with playing him straight up and delaying him until help arrives. On the first dribble, the next nearest defender (probably somewhere near half-court denying a penetrating pass to his man) sprints to the ball. Once he arrives, it is one against two, and either defender should be able to turn the ball toward the other to initiate the double team (see Diagram 5-14).

Generally, teams that use this strategy put all their hopes on beating the press on one player's shoulders. When stopped, his teammates will be in poor position to give him help. Even the most

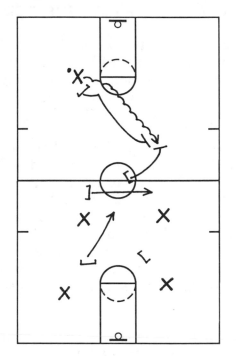

Diagram 5-14

proficient ballhandler will eventually be worn down by us to the point where two defenders can control his dribble and we can get double teams on a regular basis.

Out-of-Bounds on the Side

We have had trouble when the ball has been awarded to our opponents on the sideline in the back-court. We have found that any pass made from this position is a pass toward the middle of the court and these are the most difficult for us to react to. As a result, we are constantly caught out of position or a step behind in our rotation, and it has come to the point where we have called off "55" whenever this situation arises.

GIVING "55" A DIFFERENT LOOK

Largely because of our ineffectiveness in the sideline situation just mentioned, we have come up with an adjustment to "55" that can be implemented to give the press an entirely different look. Using the same rules of "55," we now run our press at three-quarters court ("53") and half-court ("52").

"53": All defenders back off to the foul line and do not pick up their men before this point. Any player lined up beyond the foul line falls under the jurisdiction of our press and must be covered accordingly (no penetrating passes, etc.). Once the ball crosses the foul line extended, we want it forced out of the middle. We rotate in "53" once the ball reaches the hash mark in the backcourt. On the first dribble at or beyond this hash mark, the player on the ball turns the ball back to the middle, the next defender on the weak side is the trapper, etc., similar to the rules and responsibilities of "55."

"52": All defenders back off to the hash mark, pick up their men at this point, and make their rotational moves once the ball is dribbled across half-court.

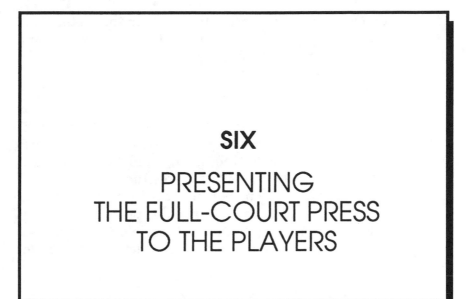

SIX

PRESENTING
THE FULL-COURT PRESS
TO THE PLAYERS

In order for our press to reach its potential level of effectiveness, it is essential that all players understand the techniques and principles involved. All players must be able to play all the defensive positions. It only takes one blown assignment to undermine the pressing effort and allow the offense an opening to get the ball downcourt. Our players are constantly reminded, "If one person fails, the press will fail." We thus spend time each and every day working on some facet of the press. Having the players master all five phases is our goal, and we demand their full commitment to this effort.

NECESSARY PLAYER ATTITUDES

Much of our pressing success relies on how it is explained by the coach and practiced by the players. The coach leaves no stone unturned and covers each phase of the press thoroughly. Any and all possibilities must be reviewed so that the players will react intelligently when confronted with similar situations in games.

The coach must also get his players to believe in the system, and to work hard to make it prosper. Along with the sweat, we demand three other characteristics of our players.

Concentration

The players must always be mentally into the game. Any lapse of concentration cannot be tolerated by the coach, and any corrections that are made must be thoroughly understood by each player. It is fairly common for us to stop a situation in practice, analyze it, then repeat it—all players must be in on this dispersal of information. We have strived to make our pressing responsibilities as simple and as consistent as possible. In return we expect that our players will focus their attention on proper execution.

Aggressiveness

As in the team man-to-man defense, we want to control the offense by making them do what we want, not what they want. Our players must be willing to outwork their opponents and not be afraid to take (intelligent) chances to reach this objective.

Intensity

This can often be the difference between success and failure during the pressing situation. Intensity refers to the pace at which the defense is played. Many teams practice the press at a controlled speed, then have trouble keeping up with the furious pace of a game. We practice at a level we expect to play in a game and demand an "intense" effort from the players each time we address this facet of our defense.

TEACHING THE PRESS

We teach our press from the whole to the part. By this, I mean that we introduce it to them in a five-on-five situation in which we introduce the five phases, show all of the movement involved, and explain the responsibilities of each position. Players digest what they can, but what is realized by all is the team concept. We want them to see that the success of the press depends on the understanding and effort of all five players on the court.

Next, we break the press down, step by step, describing to our players the expectations and opportunities that each phase affords. Each phase is its own entity, a press within the press so to speak, and we want our players to understand the intricacies of each. We have found that the best way to teach our players the details of our press is through a system of drills. These drills have been developed with the following five areas in mind:

1. Inbounds denial
2. Turning the dribbler
3. Trapping the dribbler
4. Off-the-ball rotation
5. Recovery

DRILLS TO TEACH INBOUNDS DENIAL

Three-on-three inbounds drill: Teaches inbounds denial (Guards).
See Diagram 6-1. Three offensive players line up to take the ball inbounds with their defenders assuming a position to deny this from happening. On the coach's whistle, the inbounds passer has five seconds to inbound the ball and is given the privilege of running the baseline to improve his passing angles. His defender shadows his every move during the process, staying slightly toward the inside to help protect the middle. The two offensive players looking to receive the inbounds pass do anything necessary to get open including screening, crossing, etc. We do restrict their movement in this drill, however, and allow them to move only from the baseline to the top of the key (as depicted in Diagram 6-1 by the dotted line). Any movement outside of this area in a live situation should bring help from other defenders.

In the event of a completed pass to the restricted area, we stop the drill at this point, feed the ball back out-of-bounds to the offense, find our men, and wait for the coach's whistle to restart

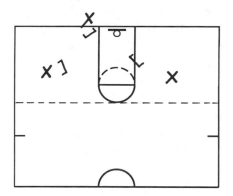

Diagram 6-1

the drill. We are concerned with developing our Phase 1 skills and use this drill solely for this purpose.

The same six players stay in the drill until the defense has prevented the inbounds pass to the area on five occasions. We have added that any completed pass to the middle, however, adds one more to this total. When the desired number of denials has been accomplished, the defense rotates off the court, the three offensive players move to defense, and a fresh trio of players take over the offensive positions.

Emphasize: Keep the first pass out of the middle, stay lower and wider than your man, hands are out and always ready.

Half-court denial drill: Teaches inbounds denial to defenders beyond the "one pass area."

The players line up on the sideline with the first player stepping out to the half-court line as the offensive player and the next man in line as his defender. A third player stands behind the baseline with the ball and attempts to pass it to the offensive player within five seconds. This player at half-court is limited to move in a section of the court as shown in Diagram 6-2. We want him to stay beyond the backcourt hash mark and out of the middle. If this man roams to these areas during a game while the ball is being taken out-of-bounds, he is getting himself out of position and we will be able to adjust to the added movement. We

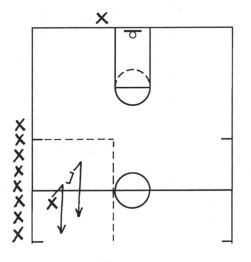

Diagram 6-2

want our players to be concerned with not letting the player receiving the inbounds pass near half-court or beyond.

On the coach's whistle, the offensive player moves to get open. His teammate out-of-bounds is not being guarded, so we have made it that much more difficult for our defender in this drill. Guarding a player so far from the ball allows this defender to sag an extra step toward the ball, making it much more difficult for his man to get between him and the ball. What the defender has to be leery of in this situation is his man going deep. We want our half-court defender to be in a position where he can see both his man and the ball. When his man starts deep, he must react and sprint down the floor with him, with the hands up and ready to go after the ball. This is a difficult pass for the offense to complete, and one that we like to see attempted (but not completed) in a game.

If the ball is deflected and knocked out-of-bounds or stolen by the defender, the drill ends and the next two players enter the court. If the pass is completed, the defender must turn his man before the front-court hash mark to end the drill, or, if this isn't possible, get in a position to stop his man from scoring as the two play one-on-one to an outcome.

Emphasize: See the ball—see your man, instant reactions—no head starts, on any lob pass find the ball and go get it.

Backdoor drill: Teaches inbounds denial techniques for players who line up in the "median strip."

See Diagram 6-3. The players line up on the sideline with two players on the court, one on offense and one as his defender. A third player stands unguarded on the baseline and will act as the passer throughout this drill. We station the offensive player at the top of the key, in what we call the median strip, and allow him to move in any direction, but tell him once he cuts deep he must keep on going and the passer must try to get him the ball. Players who line up in the median strip occasionally pose a problem for us because they are between the "one pass away" and "two passes away" areas and it is hard for us to predict what they are going to do. The defender on this player must protect against any cut to the "one pass away" area, but at the same time he must contest any lob pass thrown over the top. We are counting on our defender on the inbounds passer to make this a difficult pass; but in this drill we are going to put the defender at a disadvantage and leave the passer uncovered.

On the coach's whistle, the inbounds passer has five seconds to release the ball. His teammate at the top of the key moves right or left, and if he opens for a pass, we throw it to him, then reset the drill and insist the defender do a better job on the ensuing possession. At any time (even before the lateral cuts) the offensive player can cut deep for a pass. His defender must react to this

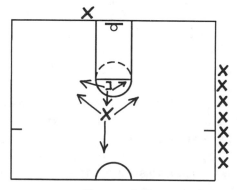

Diagram 6-3

move by getting his hands up and ready, sprinting after his man, and looking to find the ball to steal it or deflect it away. We want the passer to throw the lob, but have made a rule that this pass must be caught in the air. Back-line defenders will be there to help on overthrown lobs in game situations. If the lob pass is successful, the defender must sprint to the basket to keep his man from scoring. Whatever the outcome, these two players go to the end of the line and the front two players move out to the median strip to participate in the drill.

Emphasize: Maintain a position where you can see the ball and your man—we don't turn our backs on the ball; react instantly to deep cuts—no head starts; go after the ball—you have as much right to the ball as the offense does.

Inbounds denial drill: Teaches inbounds denial to players in the one pass away area, transition to forcing the dribble, and turning the dribbler.

See Diagram 6-4. Players line up on the sideline with the first player stepping out on defense, and the second on offense. The offensive player starts at the foul line extended and moves to get the ball in the one pass away area. The defensive player plays denial on this man and tries to steal or deflect any pass made by the coach who stands behind the baseline and acts as the inbounds passer. We restrict the offensive player to the side of the court and allow him to receive a pass anywhere before the hash

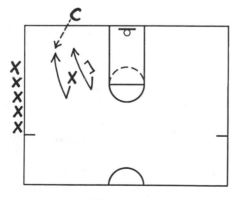

Diagram 6-4

mark. We know that any pass thrown beyond this area will bring other defenders into the picture. If a successful inbounds pass is made, the defender forces the ballhandler toward the sideline, then turns him to the middle to complete the drill. This turn must be made before the hash mark in the front court is reached by the dribbler.

We instill in our players the importance of staying in position and balanced throughout this drill. Any attempt to steal or deflect the pass must be successful; otherwise, the defender has needlessly taken himself out of position and the press is in jeopardy. As long as we force the inbounds pass to where we want it on the court, our press stays in control.

Most passes in this drill should be forced to the deep corner. If the offensive players should backdoor cut looking for a quick lob pass from the coach (completed before the hash mark), we want the defender to react, get his hands up, find the ball while sprinting after his man, and attempt to steal or deflect it. If completed, the defender takes an inside route on his man and tries to catch him and turn him before the front-court hash mark is reached. After the man is turned or the hash mark is reached, these two players go to the end of the line and the next two players jump out for their turn.

Emphasize: Proper denial stance: don't lunge, keep the weight on the balls of the feet, maintain a position where you can see both your man and the ball.

DRILLS TO TEACH TURNING THE DRIBBLER

Turning the dribbler is a skill that I underestimated in the infancy stages of developing this press. I had always assumed that players understood what was meant by "turning the dribbler" and could easily figure out the technique involved. I found out in a hurry that this is an important skill that must be taught.

Force drill: Teaches forcing the dribbler wide.

Before we turn the ball, we first want to force the dribble toward the sideline. To do this consistently, our players must be taught the correct stance for guarding the ball in a pressing situation. Like many other concepts of our press, they will find it compatible to what they have been taught in our half-court team man-to-man.

We set up this drill by lining up the players on the baseline, with two on the court—one with the ball and the other his defender. The player with the ball is standing in triple threat position in an area we want him to receive the first pass (off to the side in the "one pass away" area). The defender lines up about three feet away from his man ("close enough to touch him") with his inside foot up and wide of the ballhandler's inside foot. If this drill is run on the right side of the court (as shown in Diagram 6-5), the defender's right foot is up and outside of the ball-handler's left foot. The inside arm (right arm in this case) is held straight out at shoulder height to (1) discourage any dribble in that direction, (2) block the passing lane back to the inbounds passer, and (3) be in a position to deflect any pass attempted over the defender's head. The defender's outside arm (left arm in the diagram) points toward the sideline with the hand at the same level as the ball. If his man raises the ball to pass it, the hand mirrors the movement. If the ball is dribbled, the outside hand is ready to deflect it if not protected by the dribbler's body. The knees are bent slightly to gain a quickness advantage on the ball-handler, and the toes point forward with the weight on the balls of the feet. We maintain this stance until the ball is dribbled

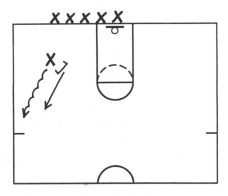

Diagram 6-5

toward the sideline. Any attempt to dribble toward the middle must be resisted with quick defensive shuffling and forced outward. When the dribble starts toward the sideline, the stance is abandoned and the defender sprints to get ahead of the ball.

Early in the season we simply have each player force his opponent to dribble wide, then stop the drill and bring the next player onto the court. As the players become skilled in our "pressing fundamentals" we add to this drill by including a passing option to the middle (to which the defender must attempt to deflect any pass in his direction), and by increasing the defensive demands to have the defender turn the dribbler before his task is complete.

Emphasize: Balanced stance, hands ready to help, react to dribble as the ball leaves the hands.

One-on-one turn drill: Teaches turning the dribbler.
See Diagram 6-6. The players line up on the baseline with the first two players moving to one side to start the drill. The offensive player stands just inbounds, holding the ball in triple threat position. The defender assumes a stance, as he would in a pressing situation, that takes away the middle and influences the dribble toward the sideline. Once the offensive player starts the dribble he must keep dribbling the entire length of the court, and we want the defender to turn him as many times as he can before they both reach the opposite baseline. At this point, the two players return to the original line, wait their turn, then switch roles the next time down the court.

Emphasize: Once the dribbler starts: turn and sprint ahead of the ball, force a reverse dribble, react quickly to any change of direction.

Note: For "Turn Drills" to achieve their intent, players must be taught the angles and technique involved in turning a dribbler.

We explain to our players that where they have taken a stance that forces the dribble toward the sideline, that is the most likely outcome. When the ball leaves the hands for the first dribble, this keys the rotation phase of our press, and we are

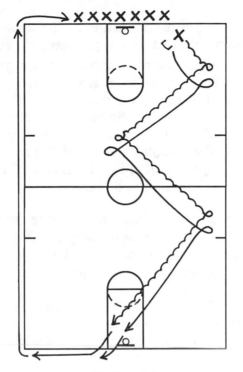

Diagram 6-6

totally reliant on this defender to turn the ball. In order to do this, he turns in the direction of the dribble and sprints along the inside of the dribbler looking to beat him to a spot on the floor. After beating the ballhandler to that spot, he then turns and faces the dribbler, moving the outside foot forward to force the dribble back to the middle. Throughout this turn, the arms are held out to the side with the forearms parallel to the floor and the hands ready to deflect any crossover dribble that is attempted in front of the body. We want the ballhandler to reverse dribble to change directions, giving us the time and angle to double team in a press situation.

All players must understand that there are two cardinal sins to be avoided when turning the dribbler:

1. *Not completing the turn.* The defender occasionally will not get his body over far enough, and this allows the dribbler to

continue forward around him and up the sideline. We tell our players, "Step out-of-bounds if you have to. Turn the ball!"

2. *Fouling.* Defenders turning the ball often grow impatient and try to beat the dribbler to a spot much too close to the ball. The result is a rub or bump with the ballhandler that is whistled as a foul on the defender. We constantly remind our players that they have all the way to the front-court hash mark to turn the dribbler. We want them to choose a spot that is far enough ahead of the dribbler so that they can get to it without contacting the dribbler.

Close-out and turn drill: Teaches approaching and turning the ball, a skill necessary to effectively carry out Phase 4.

Occasionally, an offensive player will receive the ball against our press with daylight between himself and the nearest defender. Our rule in this situation is that this nearest defender must charge at the ball, force him to dribble toward the sideline, then turn him to the middle—easier said than done. It is a skill that needs more work than words for the defenders to understand the importance of "angles" as pressing allies.

We set up this drill with a defender in the foul circle and an offensive player wide open on the side of the court (see Diagram 6-7). The coach stands behind the baseline with the ball, and the action starts when the coach throws a pass to the open player (move on the pass, not the catch!). Once the pass is received, the

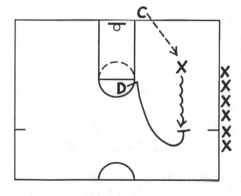

Diagram 6-7

offensive player's only option is to dribble and he is going to try and beat the defender down the sideline or back through the middle without being turned. The defender's task, obviously, is to force the dribble wide and turn the ball back to the middle. After each possession, the offensive player goes to the foul circle to be the defender on the next pass from the coach, a fresh player steps out on offense, and the defender goes to the end of the line.

To succeed in this situation, the defender must act quickly and in a manner to limit offensive choice. On the pass, he sprints directly toward the spot he would like to be in—precisely three feet away from the man's inside shoulder. If the ballhandler should delay at all (looking to make a pass, etc.), the defender would reach this area and regain control of the situation. Chances are, however, that the offensive player will feel his advantage and try to make the most of it by advancing the ball downcourt with the dribble.

As the defender sprints toward his desired spot, he must adjust to any movement the offense makes. If the man starts his dribble toward the middle, for example, the defender adjusts his sprint to a spot on the floor that he can outrace the ballhandler to and forces him to reverse his direction to the outside.

Most likely, however, the ballhandler will see the defender coming at his inside shoulder and use his dribble to advance the ball down the open sideline. This is where the defender has to understand angles. As the ball leaves the ballhandler's hands to start a dribble down the sideline, the force wide objective has been reached and the defender now concerns himself with turning the ball. He now sprints toward a spot down the sideline that he can beat the dribbler to, closing in on him all the way. Once the spot is reached, the defender turns the dribbler, and the drill is complete.

We have found that our defenders in this situation pick unrealistic spots and try to turn the dribbler long before they should. We continually remind our players that the point of the turn does not have to be in the back-court, and in the situation just described we probably won't turn the dribbler until half-court or beyond. Using the inside angle and the fact that the defender is sprinting while the ballhandler is dribbling, the defender should be able to beat the dribbler to a spot and turn him before the front-court hash mark is reached.

Emphasize: Pick a realistic spot, take a proper angle to that spot, turn the dribbler.

DRILLS TO TEACH TRAPPING

Three-man trapping drill: Teaches forcing and turning the dribbler, then trapping the ball.

We divide the players into groups of three and send them to four starting points on the court to perform the drill. Two groups will begin on opposite baselines, and the other two will begin on opposite sides of the court at the half-court stripe (see Diagram 6-8). One player in the group is the offensive player, and he holds the ball in triple threat position. The other two players are defenders, one assuming the role of man-on-the-ball, and the other is the trapper. The man-on-the-ball is in a stance to force the dribble toward the sideline. The trapper is ready to move when the dribble begins.

On the coach's whistle, the dribbler can start whenever he wants. We don't want all four groups moving on the whistle; rather we prefer that they move independently when the dribble starts in their group. Any dribble toward the middle must be denied by the man-on-the-ball and poked at by the trapper, forcing the dribbler to use the alley down the sideline. Once this avenue is taken, the man-on-the-ball sprints to beat the dribbler to a spot to turn him, while the trapper moves in to apply the double team once this is accomplished. In this drill, the defenders only have the space of a half of the court to turn and double the ball instead of all the way to the front-court hash mark that they would normally have. The dribbler wins if he can dribble past midcourt (or the baseline, depending on where he started) without being turned or doubled.

Once the dribble begins we tell the offensive player that he must move forward or laterally to keep his dribble. Any dribble backward is a victory for the defense. The defenders must realize that there are two ways the dribbler can beat them: (1) by

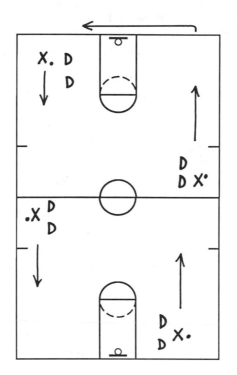

Diagram 6-8

outracing the man-on-the-ball along the sideline to half-court, and (2) by starting up the sideline and then crossing over and splitting the two defenders. Being aware of these offensive options, the man-on-the-ball not only must beat the dribbler to a spot, but must also have his hands ready to deflect any dribble made by his opponent in front of his body. The trapper, while sprinting to help, must also realize the crossover dribble as a killer to the double team and be ready to poke it from behind in the event that it is attempted. What we want in this drill is for the man-on-the-ball to beat the dribbler to a spot, turn him, force a reverse dribble, and the trapper arriving to steal the ball or double team the ballhandler if he picks up his dribble in time.

Once the double team is applied or the dribbler crosses half-court (or the baseline), the drill ends with the players moving to get ready to go at the next starting point. The three players must now rotate roles (offense to trapper to man-on-the-ball) and await the coach's whistle to signal that the dribbler can start when ready. The drill continues clockwise around the court.

Emphasize: Force the dribbler wide—no dribbles toward the middle can be allowed, force the reverse dribble.

Two-on-two trap drill: Teaches inbounds denial, forcing the dribbler wide, turning the ball, and trapping.

See Diagram 6-9. Two offensive players, one the inbounds passer and the other in the one pass away area, take the ball out-of-bounds and are defended by two players in the pressing situation. On the pass inbounds, both defenders react as they normally would while pressing. The man-on-the-ball is in a stance that influences the dribble toward the sideline. The other defender, who will be the trapper if the ball is dribbled at this point, gets in a position to deny any lateral or forward pass to his man and is ready to move if the ball is dribbled. The offensive players may pass the ball to each other, but once either puts the ball to the floor in this drill, he must try to dribble all the way beyond the front-court hash mark without being turned. The defender whose man starts to dribble must sprint to beat him to a spot while the other defender (the trapper) takes an angle to arrive at the same spot. When the turn is made, we look to get an immediate steal from the trapper. If this doesn't happen, we apply the

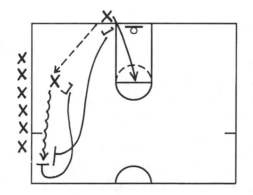

Diagram 6-9

trap to try to force the offense into a bad pass. In this drill, the offensive player is going to pass to his now unguarded teammate to conclude the drill, but we want the defenders to use their defensive advantage on the ball to make this pass a difficult one. Both sets of arms mirror the ball, and all attempts are made to steal or deflect the ball. Any turnovers will be immediately "transitioned" to the basket by the defense. If the pass out of the trap is successful, the defenders move off the court, the offensive players become the new defenders, and two new players move to the offensive positions.

Emphasize: React immediately to the first dribble, prevent the dribbler from splitting the defenders, use the arms and hands to bother the trapped opponent.

One-on-two full-court drill: Teaches turning, trapping, transition on steals, and deep man responsibilities.

See Diagram 6-10. The players arrange themselves into three lines along the baseline. The first player in the middle line steps out as the dribbler, and the first players in the other two lines move out to the elbows as defenders. On the coach's whistle, the player with the ball attempts to beat the defenders down the court with the dribble, while the defenders attempt to turn and double-team the ball, forcing a steal or picking up the dribble.

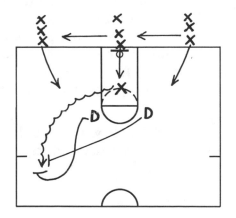

Diagram 6-10

The dribbler can go right or left, forward or backward, but must stay within the confines of the court to elude the defense. Once the ball enters the front-court, the ballhandler looks to take it to the basket for a score. After a steal, rebound, or score, the defenders take over possession and transition the ball back up the court in a two-on-one situation. This action ends with a basket, defensive rebound, or turnover. The next three players step out, take their positions, then wait for the coach's whistle. The players leaving the court move to the end of the next line on the right so that all players will get a chance to dribble and defend.

The two defenders in this drill should control the dribbler if they work together and take proper angles in their pursuit. One defender runs to a spot ahead of the ball and turns it, while the other moves in to seal the offensive player into a trap. The "turner" is responsible for preventing additional penetration down the sideline, and the trapper is concerned with not allowing dribble penetration to the middle of the floor (splitting the trap). Both defenders, especially the trapper, must move to maintain control of a dribbler who tries to back away from the trap and then attempt to circle around it.

As soon as the ball comes into the possession of the defenders, they turn to offense and the dribbler becomes the lone defender. This gives us a chance to work on the recovery phase of our press. Any defender left alone to combat a fast break opportunity must: (1) try to delay the progress of the offense for help to recover, and (2) never give up an uncontested lay-up. In order to achieve both of these objectives, this defender knows that he can never leave the lane area so that the basket remains protected, but he uses jab steps, arm fakes, or any other kinds of feints to force extra passes or dribbles to buy time to get help. Any shot taken is an assumed miss, and this defender fights to secure the rebound to end the drill.

Emphasize: Turn and double without fouling, stay in a low and wide stance until the dribble is used up, keep turning the ball until the front-court hash mark is reached.

Two-on-three drill. Teaches trapping and introduces the start of our rotation plan.

See Diagram 6-11. We start this drill by selecting six players to play offense (three groups of two) and six players to play defense (two groups of three). The offensive players line up on the baseline, while the first defensive group takes the floor and the other moves off to the sideline. We have found this drill to be less confusing when the offense and defense wear contrasting colors.

The drill starts when an offensive player grabs the ball to pass it inbounds to his teammate. One defender plays against the inbounds passer, one defender guards his inbounds teammate, and the third defender starts on the opposite wing as if he were guarding an opponent on that side of the court. The defense is obviously at an advantage in this drill, and we want this extra man situation for the defense to result in a double team and a steal to build up confidence in our pressing game. The task will obviously become more complicated as more players are added to the picture, but the defensive movement will be surprisingly similar even with five more bodies on the court.

The defense denies the inbounds pass and forces the offensive player to cut to the outside to receive the ball. Once this pass is made, our defenders react as they would under normal pressing conditions; man-on-the-ball positions himself to force any dribble wide and defenders off-the-ball sag to the line of the ball, deny any offensive players moving ahead of the ball, and are ready to move on the first dribble. Once this dribble is made, the man-on-

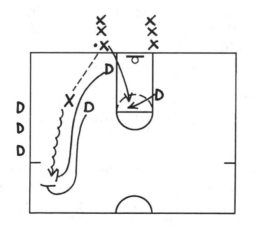

Diagram 6-11

the-ball sprints to a spot ahead of the dribbler and turns him, the next defender (the trapper) closes in for the steal or double team, and the other defender (the third man) moves to take away the passing lane to the offensive player without the ball. Any steals in the back-court are transitioned to the basket, and the same five players stay on the court. If the offense breaks the press we want them to take the ball all the way to the hoop. Play continues until a basket is scored or the defense comes up with the ball in the front-court. As soon as this happens, the whistle blows, and the action stops. One of the offensive players grabs the ball, steps behind the baseline, and the same two groups repeat the drill back up the court. At the conclusion of this second possession, the defensive groups switch and the next two offensive players step forward to try to beat the pressure.

Emphasize: All defenders move when the ball leaves the dribbler's hands; man-on-the-ball must complete the turn, trapper prevents the dribbler from splitting the trap; if first trap is broken, move to turn and double again.

DRILLS TO TEACH ROTATION

Five-on-five walk-through drill. Teaches the rotation process of our press.

Perhaps the best way to teach our rotation system to our players is by setting up a five-on-five situation, then going through all the different possibilities that may occur. In this drill, five offensive players are selected and then positioned on the floor in what we consider normal pressbreaking positions. Next we pick five defenders and assign each to an offensive player. We continually vary the offensive positioning until we have covered all the pressbreaking alignments we figure that we will see during the course of the season.

On the coach's command, the ball is passed inbounds to a player in the one pass away area. The man-on-the-ball gets into a stance to force the dribble wide while his four teammates assume a position to deny any penetrating pass. The coach will then call out a situation, such as "Dribble up the sideline," or "Pass it back to the inbounds passer," or "Pass it crosscourt to Jeff," with the offense carrying out the assignment and the defense reacting to the ball and situation. Any time the ball is dribbled, we want to end up with two players trapping the ball, two other players in a position to steal passes out of the trap, and one player protecting the basket. We allow no steals (or "dummy heroes") during this drill and ask that the defense concentrate on position and responsibility and save their aggressiveness for live action.

After repositioning the offense and talking them through some more situations, we look to challenge the defensive players' understanding of our rotation. The coach takes the offense aside and choreographs offensive patterns which the defense must stop. All through the implementation of these patterns we are looking to see if the defensive players make proper decisions in attacking the ball and rotating to proper positions.

To make sure that the players themselves are making the proper decisions, the coach should be careful not to call out instructions for the defense every time a decision has to be made. The coach must allow his players to make mistakes so that they can learn from these and be ready to think for themselves once they are in a game situation. When mistakes are made in this drill (and a clever coach can cause many), we have the players tell the coach what went wrong or how the situation should have been handled differently. After these determinations, we repeat the situation and the defense now adjusts in a more sensible and effective manner.

Emphasize: Players must concentrate at all times: think ahead, anticipate what the player with the ball might do.

Three-on-four drill. Teaches turning the dribble, double teaming the ballhandler, and proper rotation.

See Diagram 6-12. We start this drill by selecting six players to play offense (two groups of three) and then choosing four of the remaining players to play defense. Any excess players (usually two) side with the defense and will rotate in between possessions. With the number of players involved and the fact that players on the court are constantly changing, it becomes a necessity in this drill for the offense and defense to wear contrasting colors.

CHAPTER SIX

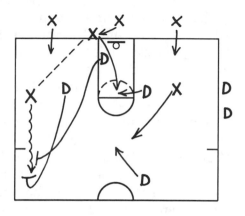

Diagram 6-12

The objective for the offensive players is to beat the four defenders up the court for a shot at the basket. The defenders, in turn, must use the concepts of our press to stop the offense and force a turnover. We initiate the drill by giving the ball to an inbounds passer and telling his two teammates to get open. One defender plays against the inbounds passer, two others guard his teammates, and the fourth defender assumes the role of stealer, and lines up at half court ready to take any cutter that goes deep or move to pick off any lob pass thrown inbounds. Once the ball is successfully inbounded, the rules of the press take hold, with the man-on-the-ball forcing the dribbler wide then turning him into a double team with the two defenders off the ball moving to logical passing outlets. With only two players to cover, their decision is an easy one and the defense should have some success in this format. Any time in this drill that the ball is stolen in the back court, the defense takes the ball right back to the hoop and we start the drill over.

If the press is beaten, the defenders sprint back to the lane, then pick up their men. The offense challenges this half-court defense in a three-on-four situation with the extra defender (originally, the stealer) staying in the middle near the basket looking to help on any penetration. Play continues until a basket is scored or the defense comes up with the ball in the front-court.

At this point the possession ends, the ball is dropped, and we immediately start a second possession with the same seven players back down the court. An offensive player grabs the ball and steps out-of-bounds, the defenders find their men, and the stealer gets to a position where he can support his teammates. The same rules apply on this possession, and when it comes to a conclusion back where we started, we change offensive groups and rotate in new defensive players.

Emphasize: The man-on-the-ball must turn the dribbler (no deep man support); any pass thrown is a potential steal, turn steals into quick baskets.

Anticipation drill. Teaches off-the-ball defenders to read the passer and to anticipate passing options.

See Diagram 6-13. This drill starts by dividing the players into three groups of four. The first group sets up on defense, the next group plays offense, and the final group waits on the baseline for their chance to rotate in. The ball starts inbounds with all four defenders assuming proper pressing alignments and the ball-handler dribbling up the sideline purposely into a trap. This now leaves the third man and the stealer as the "interceptors" and three offensive players off-the-ball to guard, so they must develop

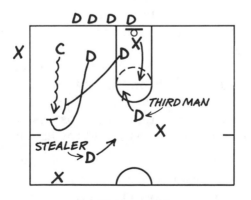

Diagram 6-13

a sense of anticipation to be in the right place at the right time. This is what this drill is all about.

Early in the season we displace the ballhandler with the coach. The coach then "telegraphs" and lobs passes out of the trap to give the interceptors initial success. This helps to create confidence, which is an important building block to the success of our press. Slowly, the passes become more precise and increasingly difficult to defend, but with a growing awareness of anticipation our defenders will "make the play" more times than not. Interceptors learn how to read the passer's eyes, understand the body language that helps predict when and where the pass will be made, and eventually think right along with the ballhandler as to what is the best pass available and step in and take it away. We teach our interceptors to be active and deceptive—active to cover three passing lanes with two people, and deceptive to make passing options look open, yet when attempted within reach of a defensive steal.

As the season wears on and our interceptors become adept at anticipating the pass out of the trap, the coach retreats to the sideline and brings in the fourth offensive player as the ballhandler. We have found that using a player as the ballhandler early in the season tends to overmatch the defense and destroys confidence instead of building it up.

Any time the defense steals the ball in this drill, we want them to turn it into a quick basket. If the pass out of the double team is successful, the player receiving the pass immediately dribbles down the court. The nearest defender must charge the ball, force it wide, and then turn it back to the middle before the front-court hash mark to conclude the possession. If this doesn't occur and the press is beaten, the offense goes to the basket and the possession ends on a basket or defensive possession. After each possession, the ball is thrown back to the coach (or given to the ballhandler), the same two groups line up and the drill is repeated. After a selected number of possessions, the groups rotate from offense to defense to behind the baseline.

Emphasize: Trappers: get a piece of the pass; Interceptors: be aggressive and not afraid to take chances; whenever the ball gets behind you turn and sprint down the court to help out recovery.

Combination drill. Teaches the fundamental skills involved in pressing (turning, trapping, rotating) as well as reviewing team man-to-man concepts in the front-court.

In this drill we combine the concepts of our press with those of the team man-to-man defense so that our players can view both systems as a "defensive package" and not as two separate entities thrown together. We start the drill by lining up the players on the baseline and then selecting two players to play defense, one in the back-court and the other in the front-court. This is the one-on-one phase of our combination drill (see Diagram 6-14). To help with the rotation of this drill we also select a player as the "on-deck defender," and he moves to the sideline near where the dribble is started. The players will then rotate from offense to on-deck defender to back-court defender to front-court defender to the end

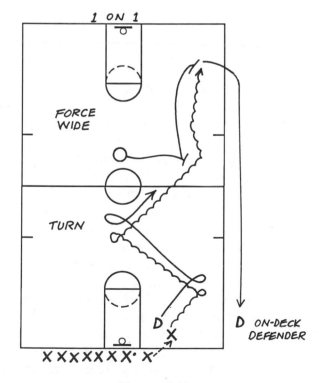

Diagram 6-14

of the line on succeeding possessions. Also, the next player on the baseline has a ball to eliminate wasted time between possessions.

The drill starts with the offensive player trying to advance the ball upcourt with the dribble. The back-court defender tries to turn the ball as many times as possible until it gets to half-court. Once this line is reached, the back-court defender is done and the front-court defender picks up the ballhandler and is governed by our team man-to-man defensive rules. The two play one-on-one to a conclusion, with the action ending on a basket or defensive possession. The defender then takes the ball back down the sideline with him while the offensive player heads to the on-deck line. During this time the defenders have rotated in and the next player on the baseline steps out and starts his dribble up the court. We run this drill through until everybody has had a chance to defend in both the back-court and the front-court.

Next, we tell the players "two-on-two" (see Diagram 6-15), and run the same drill with the same rotation, only this time we add a player to the offense and to the defense. The offense now takes the ball out-of-bounds, and the back-court defenders are responsible for denying the inbounds pass and then turning and doubling the dribble. This will leave the other offensive player wide open for a pass in this drill. We are not looking for steals here, but rather forcing the ballhandler to give up the ball. We know the steals will come in a five-on-five situation. Once the offense crosses half-court, they are met by two more defenders who play them by our team man-to-man rules.

Once all the players have had a chance to defend in the two-on-two situation, we establish a three-on-three phase of the drill (see Diagram 6-16). We use the same rules and the same rotation, but with four groups we have to eliminate the on-deck line, and players on offense must now move quickly back up the court after their possession to take over as back-court defenders. We look for the back-court defenders to deny the inbounds pass, force any dribble wide, turn and double the dribbler, then look to steal the pass out of the trap with the "interceptor" off-the-ball. Any steal is taken to the basket and the possession is restarted. If the press is beaten, the offense is met by three front-court defenders who pick them up using our team man-to-man rules.

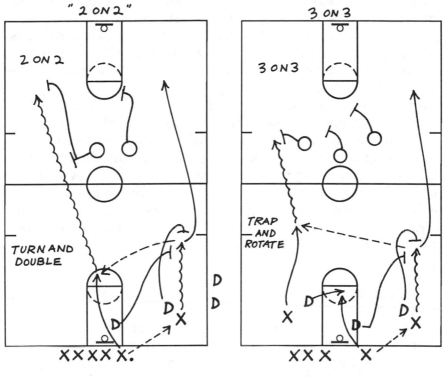

Diagram 6-15   Diagram 6-16

Emphasize: Concentrate: know the situation, turn back-court steals into baskets; front-court defenders must communicate when picking up their men.

DRILLS TO TEACH RECOVERY

We realize that during the course of each game we are going to occasionally find ourselves in shorthanded situations, so we prepare for this occurrence daily. We consider this the final phase of our press, but also realize that we may end up shorthanded for a lot of reasons other than teams breaking our press. Teams that fast break off the defensive rebound or that transition steals into fast break opportunities must be defended by our "recovery phase" concepts. We view any drill work done on this phase of our press as doubly important: (1) to provide a solid last line of defense for our press, and (2) to react to any transition situation to "Stop the Ball" (team man-to-man rule 1) to allow our half-court defense to go into effect.

One important factor we tell our players about this final phase of our press is that even when teams beat our press and break to the basket, our press is still in effect. More often than not, the guards have given up the ball and this final break is composed of the "big men" handling the ball and moving to the basket—certainly not the way teams practice the fast break. We feel that with our deep man, conditioned to slow up the action and force mistakes, and a hustling quartet of recovering teammates, we can still force turnovers or bad shots even when it appears that the offense has the advantage.

Deep man drill.   Teaches protecting the basket in a two-on-one situation.

See Diagram 6-17. Players are divided up into four groups of three. One group is designated the "deep man" group and they move to line up at the hash mark in the front-court. Another group is chosen to be the "rebounding" group, and they remain on the baseline in the back-court. The final two groups are the "fast break" groups and line up at each hash mark in the back-court. The coach stands near the foul line and starts the drill by shooting and missing. The first rebounder in line gets the ball and outlets it to the player in front of the fast break line on the side of the rebound. The fast break player on the opposite hash mark cuts to the middle, receives a pass from the outlet, and the two break downcourt in a two-on-one situation. The deep man starts on the sideline, breaks to the center circle on the coach's shot, then backpedals to the basket and analyzes the situation. We want the offense to get a good, quick shot, and at the same time demand that the deep man not allow this to happen. We encourage him to jab step to the ball and retreat or to do anything in his power to confuse the offense without fouling or leaving the lane. All shots must be contested—we cannot allow free lay-ups.

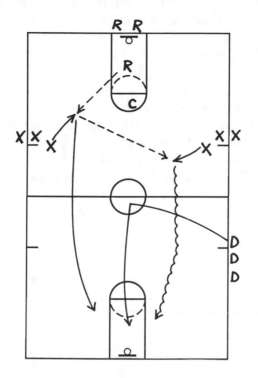

Diagram 6-17

Once the ball comes into the deep man's possession or the offense scores, these three players move off the court and return to the end of the next line in the rotation pattern. The drill is repeated until all of our players have had a chance to be the deep man.

Emphasize: Defender must go straight up on all shots—no fouls; do anything to slow down the ball—deflect it, kick it, draw the charge.

Decision drill. Teaches the deep man when to go after the long pass and when to protect the basket.

See Diagram 6-18. We start this drill by dividing the players into three groups of four and lining up one group on the baseline (the deep men) and the other two on each sideline (the offensive players). The first player in each line steps out, with the deep man moving to the foul line and each offensive player somewhere near the foul line extended. The coach has the ball in the back-court and is going to attempt to pass to either offensive player (each is active on his own side of the court) to set up a two-on-one break. The deep man must decide on the pass whether to go after it or retreat to the basket. If the pass has enough loft or is thrown close enough for him to get it, we want the deep man to be aggressive and go get it. If the pass is thrown on a line or at an angle that would be difficult to intercept, we want the deep man to get into position to protect the basket. Any completed pass results in a

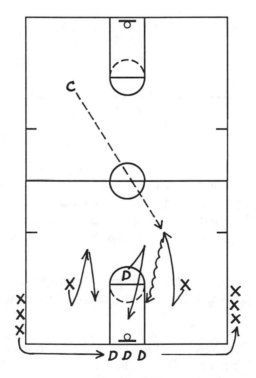

Diagram 6-18

two-on-one break to the basket, while any intercepted or broken up pass ends the drill and sends all three players to the end of their next line.

This is the type of pass that might be thrown out of a trapping situation, and we want our players to realize that any long pass is open game and ours if we are ready to react. For this reason, the coach must vary the loft and angle of his passes to force the deep man to make decisions. If he feels he can outrace the offensive player to the ball, he should go for it. If there is doubt, he should back off to the basket and implement the recovery phase of our press, which starts with his attempt to delay the break.

Emphasize: Make a decision and live with it—don't get caught in between; if there is any doubt, retreat to the hoop.

Three-on-two drill (with trailer). Teaches the tandem defense used when faced with a shorthanded situation.

See Diagram 6-19. We run this continuous fast break drill almost every day, both to work on our fast breaking skills and the shorthanded defensive situation with recovery help on the way. This is a practical situation in that the stealer and deep man are sometimes caught back together in an attempt to fend off a three-on-two break. This is what has been set up in this drill. Three players head to the basket in a fast break situation against two defenders, and as soon as the ball crosses half-court, a third defender enters from the sideline, touches the center circle, then sprints to the basket to find the open man. If the defenders can slow down the ball and not allow a quick shot, it is then a three-on-three situation. Once defensive possession is secured or the offense scores, the three defensive players turn to offense and bring the ball down the court against two more defenders waiting for them at the other end. As soon as they cross half-court, a third defender sprints out, touches the center circle, and the drill is repeated.

It is important that our players understand tandem defense and are able to use it effectively to slow down the ball in a three-on-two situation. The two defenders must communicate as to who is out front. We don't want two defenders standing side-by-side as the ball approaches the scoring area. One player must

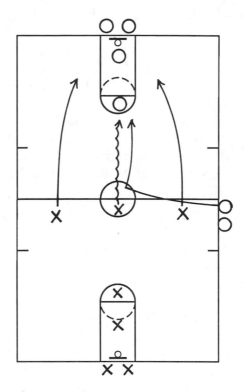

Diagram 6-19

assume the "I've got ball!" role out front, and it is his job to stop
the ball out near the foul line. If this is done and a pass is made
to a wing, the back defender attacks this wing while the foul line
defender slides down to protect the basket. If the original ballhandler tries to drive to the basket, the man out front forces him
wide, stays with him, and the back man protects opposite—shutting off any passing lane near the basket. These two defenders
must maintain proper positioning and work to prevent easy
lay-ups. We tell them that if they can force the offense to use more
than one pass, then they have bought the time necessary to bring
recovering teammates into the picture.

Emphasize: Stop the ball: force the ballhandler to pick up his dribble, defenders must react to the pass when it leaves the passer's hands, assume a miss on every shot and go get the ball.

AFTERWORD

We have used the "team man-to-man" defense along with its full-court complement quite successfully over the past seven seasons. Where other teams spend time on developing a myriad of defenses, we have found that simplifying the situation and giving our full attention to just one defensive philosophy works just fine for us. Our time is spent developing this one system of defense, and we know that as a result we will apply a more coordinated, effective pressure than our opponents, who are sharing their practice time between several defensive schools of thought.

This does not mean that the only way this system can work is to scrap all other defensive ideas and work solely within this system. The point is that the effectiveness of the defense is a result of the time spent learning and practicing it. Some coaches like to mix up zones and man-to-man, and I profess to them that this would be an ideal man-to-man supplement to the zone philosophy. A lot of what has been written in this book has familiar tones for the coach who likes zones. It is my personal belief that zones alone can't provide a strong enough defensive arsenal to win the tough battles. For the coach who plays straight man-to-man and relies on the athletic ability of each of his players to stop their individual opponents, I invite him to take a look at this philosophy as a way to get even more out of that athletic ability. The team man-to-man defense has worked for us, and coaches who are willing to invest time and energy with this philosophy will find that it will work for them as well.

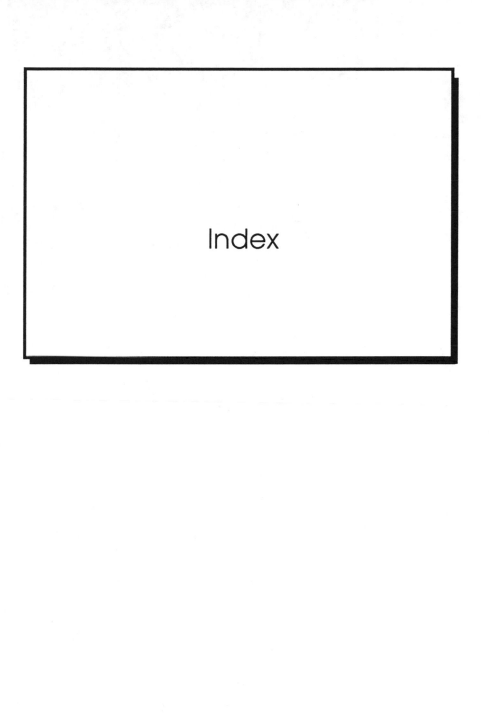

Index

E